Turning Toys

with Richard Raffan

Turning Toys
with Richard Raffan

The Taunton Press

The Taunton Press
Inspiration for hands-on living®

The Taunton Press, Inc.,
63 South Main Street, PO Box 5506, Newtown, CT 06470-5506
e-mail: tp@taunton.com

Editors: David Heim, Christina Glennon
Copy Editor: Seth Reichgott
Indexer: Jay Kreider
Cover Designer: carol singer | notice design
Interior Designer: Rosalind Loeb Wanke
Layout Artist: Tinsley Morrison
Photographer: All photos by Richard Raffan except for the top photos on p. 99 by Richard Heddington LRPS.
Illustrator: Melanie Powell

The following manufacturers/names appearing in *Turning Toys* are trademarks: Dremel®,
Henry Taylor®, Velcro®

Library of Congress Cataloging-in-Publication Data

Raffan, Richard.
 Turning toys / Richard Raffan.
    pages cm
 Includes bibliographical references and index.
 ISBN 978-1-62113-010-9 (paperback)
 1. Wooden toys. 2. Toy making. 3. Woodwork. 4. Turning (Lathe work) I. Title.

TT174.5.W6R34 2013
745.592–dc23

Printed in the United States of America

10 9 8 7 6 5 4 3 2 1

ABOUT YOUR SAFETY

Working with wood is inherently dangerous. Using hand or power tools improperly or ignoring safety practices can lead to permanent injury or even death. Don't try to perform operations you learn about here (or elsewhere) unless you're certain they are safe for you. If something about an operation doesn't feel right, don't do it. Look for another way. We want you to enjoy the craft, so please keep safety foremost in your mind whenever you're in the shop.

Acknowledgments

Before I tackled this book, the only toys I'd made were sets of spillikins (pick-up sticks) and spinning tops. It's unlikely I'd have undertaken *Turning Toys* of my own volition, so I'm very grateful to Peter Chapman, who suggested the project and signed me up.

My thanks go to Jane McClintock, a niece and mother of two small boys, who provided some useful insights into how children play and respond to a range of toys and games.

For me, the creation of *Turning Toys* became a stimulating 3-month challenge that involved 12- to 14-hour days of writing, photography, a long-suffering but supportive wife, and even a bit of woodturning. Throughout those hectic weeks, David Heim provided an enjoyable and accommodating editing experience, making *Turning Toys* a better book than it might have been.

Contents

INTRODUCTION   2

1   SAFE DESIGN   4

2   TOOLS   8

3   WOOD & PREPARING BLANKS   17

4   THINGS WE FORGET (BUT SHOULDN'T)   24

5   TURNING CYLINDERS & DOWELS   30

6   TURNING WHEELS   40

PROJECTS   54

7   WHEELY BUG   56

8   RACING CAR   65

9   PEGGIES   72

10   WANDS   80

11   STACKERS   88

12   SPHERES   98

13   FRUIT & VEGETABLES TO "CUT"   106

14   CROQUET SET   115

15   TEETHER & RATTLE   122

16   NESTING TUBS   131

17   GOBLET   139

18   BILBOQUET   146

19   SPINNING TOPS   152

20   BALANCE TRAY   159

21   TABLE SKITTLES   166

FINAL TOUCHES   176

FURTHER READING   183

INDEX   184

Introduction

This is a book about toys and games for kids that you can turn on a lathe. It's nearly impossible to come up with anything new in this area, given that humans have been making toys for kids for thousands, and possibly tens of thousands, of years. My intention is to provide a clutch of projects that are quirky variations on traditional themes, at the same time offering you some wonderful skill-building exercises for which a big lathe and fancy tools are not required.

Almost every project has been turned and photographed on my smallish Vicmarc 150 lathe, seen in its entirety on p. 13. The VL150 swings 11¾ in. (300mm) and accommodates 13¾ in. (350mm) between centers. To make the book comprehensible to readers everywhere, measurements throughout the book are in both metric and imperial and for the most part are rounded up to the nearest ⅛ in. or 5mm.

The projects will teach you about chucking and measuring and will develop your tool technique. My aim is to provide you with more than a set of designs or plans to follow. This is an ideas and techniques book, so once you have the principle of how to go about it, you can take an idea and make your own version. Many of the skills you learn here can be applied to a wide variety of jobs on the lathe. I've included simple techniques for mounting wood, some you might not have thought of. There are ideas for enhancing a basic turning with carving, staining, drawing, and painting.

Photos and a few drawings show you what to do, step by step; you'll see exactly how the tools are used, how the cutting edge should relate to the surface you're cutting, and the sort of shavings you can expect when everything is going well. In the text I warn you of potential problems and offer ways to circumvent them.

My aim is to give you more than enough information to overcome the problems you'll run into as you work through each project. Many of them may appear similar, but each offers its own set of challenges. If you want to learn about turning in greater depth, I refer you to the Further Reading list on p. 183.

Even if you don't have kids in your life, a son or daughter, niece or nephew, grandchild, or even brother or sister, there are lots of kids out there with nobody to make stuff for them. You can make as many toys and games as you like knowing that, sadly, there are millions of kids who would be delighted to have anything you've made. You can reach those kids through charitable organizations and church groups, who always welcome anything that might enrich the lives of the kids they help.

Repetition is the key to mastering any craft, and toys tend to involve lots of repetition in the form of wheels, beads, and spindles. You can get plenty of practice executing simple projects for small kids, who can't have too many peg dolls, balls, and things on wheels. With practice, you'll discover ways of salvaging a situation when things go wrong, as they inevitably do. Turn disasters into design opportunities, keeping in mind that often what looks like a disaster to an adult doesn't faze a child at all.

When I first came up with possible projects for this book, I was thinking of the objects I could make for kids rather than how I'd make them. I knew they would be round and that was about it. I soon realized that almost every project involved some form of spindle turning and, consequently, the use of a skew chisel, a tool that scares the daylights out of many a novice turner. Needlessly, I might add. The skew chisel catches that unnerve most novice turners, those that happen when turning spindles, are rarely dangerous; mostly they just mess up the wood. The dangerous and occasionally life-threatening catches are those involving scrapers and gouges on platters and bowls nearing completion. It is those catches that often result in serious injury, trips to the hospital, and stitches.

If you are new to woodturning, the best thing you can do is come to terms with skew chisels by spending time turning some sort of spindle. This book is full of projects that are ideal for anyone in need of skew-chisel practice—and that's all of us. Skew-chisel practice is to a woodturner what scales are to a musician.

Finally, anything that survives being used by one generation has a good chance of being tucked away in a box for the next. Few things are more satisfying than making gifts for people you know, let alone love, especially when you can watch them using and enjoying the products of your labors. My hope is that this book will help you spend many happy and fruitful hours at your lathe, interspersed with some quiet times painting and decorating, creating heirlooms for your succeeding generations.

1 SAFE DESIGN

W e tend to forget that toys and games have as much to do with learning and skill-building as they do with play. Most childhood games help develop our minds, dexterity, hand—eye coordination, and life skills. Think of games that involve counting, like hide-and-seek or sardines, or games that develop our ability to control our limbs, like hopscotch. We develop hand skills by stacking blocks and threading beads. Games once provided the groundwork that enabled us to survive as hunter-gathers in a hostile environment. They still do, although the hunting and gathering is

EYE-CATCHING.
Color attracts toddlers and adds an element that older kids can use when inventing games.

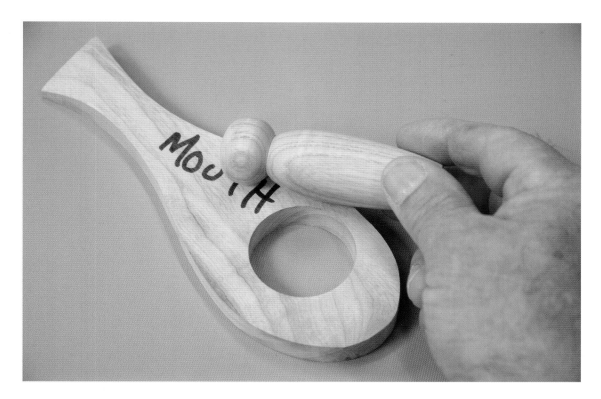

SAFETY TESTER.
I use this homemade gauge to find out if pieces are small enough for a toddler to swallow. Anything that goes through the 1¾-in. (45mm) hole, no matter how it's presented, poses a choking hazard.

now in a different sort of hostile environment. That's the first clutch of stuff to bear in mind when you design and make toys.

Next, remember that if you want an object tested to destruction, children are up to the task. Kids are forever learning something new about the world, their environment, and the objects it contains. Many of the projects in this book are designed to withstand the rigors of life with a 2- or 3-year-old who constantly seeks and discovers boundaries and wants answers to barely formulated questions: How hard can I whack this before it breaks? Will it break if I bash it on the floor? I wonder what it tastes like? As you design and create your own variations of these projects, remember that small kids tend to stick things in their mouths before bashing them repeatedly against the floor to see what happens. That is partly why toys for small kids are chunky.

When you're making stuff for toddlers who are still learning the names of colors and devel-oping motor skills as they sort shapes and sizes, it's a good idea to use color whenever possible. Then you can suggest a red, blue, or green ball or cup when they are assembling a building toy like the nesting tubs on p. 131.

Toy Safety for Toddlers

When you design toys, it's wonderful to end up with something that looks great, feels good, and does what it is supposed to do. Wheels need to spin and balls must roll with reasonable accuracy, but overriding all that is safety.

AVOID CHOKING HAZARDS

It seems that until the age of 3 we all have an innate desire to stick things in our mouths. That makes choking an ever-present possibility. You need to ensure that components like beads and wheels won't fit in a small mouth if they break loose.

Many countries have strict safety regulations for toys sold in stores. You'll find the regulations

SHARP POINTS. Kids aged 7 to 12 are brilliant at picking one stick off the pile without disturbing those below, but they need supervision to prevent sticks from being broken. Those pointy ends are a hazard for toddlers.

on the Internet. These standards don't apply to toys you make at home, but it's well worth following them as a matter of common sense. In U.S. stores and on the Internet, you can purchase inexpensive no-choke testing tubes. These vary from 1¼ in. (32mm) to 1½ in. (38mm) in diameter and 2¼ in. (57mm) to 2¾ in. (70mm) deep. Any object that fits entirely within the tube can be considered a choking hazard. My homemade gauge, shown on p. 5, is a 1¾-in.-wide hole in a scrap of hardwood. If a part goes through the hole no matter how it's presented, I regard it as too small.

KEEP MAGNETS IN PLACE
Very strong rare-earth magnets are wonderful for holding parts together, like the fruit in Chapter 13, but they have been cited as a major hazard in the home now that they are commonplace in toys. If a child swallows a magnet, then a short time later swallows another or a small steel object, these could snap together and block the intestine. If you use magnets in toys, they must be glued in place with epoxy so they *never* come loose. Also, the part holding the magnet must be too large to swallow.

BLUNT SHARP POINTS
One of the responsibilities of being an adult caring for kids is to keep some toys out of the wrong (tiny) hands. Delicate stuff like spillikins (more prosaically called pick-up sticks) needs to be kept from toddlers who would almost certainly break them and injure themselves with the pointy ends. Spillikins are fragile, so young kids need to be supervised while playing that game and taught not to squeeze the sticks together so much that they break.

In general, toys can do without sharp edges and corners that can break skin if whacked against an arm in a tantrum. Think rounded corners rather than sharp angles. Remember, too, that rounded corners are less likely to splinter when knocked hard.

BE SMOOTH

Make sure you sand all surfaces smooth and that there are no potential splinters. Where there is a split on a corner or rim, insert a blade or chisel and pry the splinter free or fill the gap with epoxy so the splinter never comes loose. If you run your hand against the grain, you'll soon discover any problem areas.

Smooth does not necessarily mean ultrafine. Sanding with 120-grit can often be more than sufficient, as it is with most balls, where heavy sanding distorts the sphere.

Size, Scale, and Weight

Toys need to be the right size for the hands playing with them. If you're going to invest a lot of time making something, it's a good idea to do a rough version first to see if the size is right for the recipient. Making a mock-up also gives you a better understanding of any problems in turning or assembly.

Children's versions of games like croquet and skittles need to be scaled down from the adult variety. Balls, for instance, need to be sized for a particular age group, so if you're turning balls for a family game, think of varying the size and weight.

Toddlers' toys need to be light in weight, so if a wood feels heavy to you (as an adult), it's probably worth using in only small quantities. A racing car in cocobolo, ironwood, or African blackwood might look wonderful, but might be heavier than a toddler ought to be lifting at that age. Better are lighter hardwoods like elm, poplar, or cherry, or hard softwoods like some of the good-quality pines.

SCALE. Mock-ups like these car bodies help you decide the ideal size for your design. You also get to practice cuts and chucking techniques.

2 TOOLS

This chapter gives you a brief rundown of the tools you'll need for the projects in this book. All the tools shown in the photos are widely available from woodturning and woodworking retailers at their stores, from their catalogs, or online.

You can easily spend a small fortune on woodturning tools and widgets. You need only three basic tools for most of these projects, but a few more can make life easier. A mini-lathe will suffice for most of the projects.

For more information and deeper insights regarding tools and techniques, I refer you to my other books, in which I have written in depth on most aspects of turning wood. You might also find my videos helpful. (See p. 183 for a list of titles.)

Gouges, Skew Chisels, and Scrapers

You can turn wood on almost any sort of lathe, but if you don't have decent tools to cut the wood, you're on a hiding to nothing—in a hopeless situation. For these projects you can manage with the four in the photo on the facing page. With these tools you can turn almost everything from spindles with beads and grooves to small bowls and boxes. Each tool has a classic shape that professional toolmakers and woodturners have refined over generations. If I could afford

only one tool, though, it would be the $\frac{1}{2}$-in. (13mm) spindle gouge, because with it I can turn almost anything.

One good tool that holds an edge is worth a hundred that don't. The best tools are made of high speed steel (HSS). These vary in type and hardness from M2 to A11, M4, ASP 2030 and 2060, and Kryo steels. (Those designations are shorthand for the steel's composition and the way it is hardened.) Most of my tools are made of Kryo or M2. These metals hold an edge far longer than the old carbon-steel tools that were the norm until the 1980s. Those old tools, which you can still find at garage sales and flea markets, are ideal starting tools but will need sharpening often. In the 1970s, when I was turning a lot of teak, I reckoned a carbon-steel gouge would last only about 8 months because I had to sharpen it so often.

Avoid sets of very inexpensive tools because they are rarely worth the box that holds them. Many fail to hold an edge for more than a few seconds, even if they claim to be HSS. Toolmakers in Sheffield, England, continue to produce some of the best woodturning tools. The names to look for are Henry Taylor®, Robert Sorby, and Hamlet. The products from American manufacturers Thompson Lathe Tools and D-Way Tools are also as good as you can get.

You may be tempted to try scraping tools with disposable cutters that claim to make turning easy. These can indeed remove a lot of wood very quickly with fewer catches, but I still prefer traditional gouges and skew chisels. Carbide scrapers can never produce as smooth a surface on spindles and other centerwork as traditional tools do, so you'll spend many more hours sanding than you need. In most situations, you get a much better surface by shear-cutting with traditional tools, although that requires practice. And that is partly what these pages aim to provide, along with guidance as to how to use the tools.

Sharpening

Tools made of the very best steel are of no use unless they are sharp—and you must be able to maintain that sharpness. If it even vaguely crosses your mind that a gouge or skew chisel could be sharper, go straight to the grindstone and touch up the edge. With some woods, you may have to sharpen the tool every few seconds; with other woods, the same tool may stay sharp for days.

Most woodturners use an inexpensive high-speed grinder fitted with composite abrasive wheels manufactured specifically for high-speed steel. The typical grinder has a coarse 46-grit wheel on one side for rough grinding and shaping, and a finer 80-grit wheel on the other side for refining the edge. I use edges straight off the finer grinding wheel, rarely honing a gouge or skew chisel because the resulting microbevel can make the tools tricky to use.

The grinding wheel shown on the pages that follow is a CBN (cubic boron nitride) wheel that I began using only a few months ago; I can't see myself reverting to composite grinding wheels. CBN wheels cut quickly but with less heat buildup than composite wheels. They are solid steel and don't shrink with use, so you never need to adjust jigs and rests once they are set up. Composite wheels gradually become smaller as the abrasive wears away. Being solid steel, CBN wheels shouldn't fly apart and so can remain unshielded. Composite wheels should always be used with a shield because they can disintegrate. As always with any spinning object, you must guard against your clothing, your hair, your tie, or anything else snagging in the wheel.

BASIC FIRST STEPS

To prepare a tool for grinding, remove any burr by honing the top of a scraper or the flute of a gouge. A small roll of 180-grit abrasive, preferably cloth-backed, is ideal for honing a gouge because with pressure it will flex to fit the entire flute.

When grinding as when turning, the key is not to push the tool against the wheel but to let it rest on the wheel. Think of this as letting the wheel come to the tool, not pushing the tool into the wheel. The grinding will raise a small burr, but it vanishes once the tool starts cutting.

SCRAPERS AND SKEWS

Scrapers and skew chisels are easy to sharpen freehand if you have an adjustable platform rest like the one shown below. Set the rest at the angle you need and keep the tool flat on the rest as you grind. When sparks come over the edge of the tool, it should be sharp and have a single bevel like the skew chisel in the photo on p. 9 and the middle gouge in the photo at right. That said, when you're sharpening on CBN and other wheels designed specifically for high-speed steel, there won't be many sparks. Instead, watch the bright edge, seen on the right half of the edge in

PROPER AND IMPROPER GRINDS. The gouge in the middle has a single bevel—a sign that it has been sharpened correctly. The faceted bevel on the bottom gouge is all right, too. But the steep secondary bevel on the top tool—it shows as a narrow white line at the cutting edge—will make it hard to use.

the photo below. When that darkens, as on the left side, the edge should be sharp.

Skew chisels are also held flat on the rest, as shown in the top left photo on the facing page. I like my skew edges to have a slight radius for peeling cuts (see the bottom photo on p. 36). To produce that edge, I swing the handle sideways a few degrees. Anything but straight will do. Notice, too, that the rounded side of the tool blade is flattened between the two bevels. This has two benefits. First, you create a much sharper corner or long point. Second, you'll be able to use the bevel side to achieve an exceptionally clean cut on endgrain.

GOUGES

Sharpening gouges freehand is fast, but it's an art that needs a bit of practice. The tool must be able to pivot on a narrow rest, so tilt the platform rest so it is nearly vertical. Move the heel of

STABLE PLATFORM. A large stable tool rest is essential for supporting skew chisels and scrapers when you sharpen them freehand with a grinder.

SHARPENING A SKEW. When the side of a skew chisel is rounded, flatten the end between the two bevels. The bright triangle between the bevels was created on the side of the grinding wheel.

the gouge to touch the grinding wheel, then raise the tool handle to ease the remainder of the bevel against the wheel. When the sparks come over the edge or the edge changes color very slightly, begin to grind the wing by easing the gouge up the wheel as you roll it onto its side (see the photos at right). To avoid flat spots on the edge, you need to keep the gouge moving. Having done one wing, reverse the action keeping the edge on the wheel and do the other side.

With practice, you can touch up the edge of a gouge in about 5 seconds. Don't worry if you fail to get a single bevel like the one shown in the center of the top photo on the facing page; the ⅛-in.-wide (3mm) bevel from the edge on the lower gouge is fine. It doesn't look pretty, but it works. What makes the top gouge difficult to use is the steep and very small bevel along the cutting edge.

A grinding jig like the one shown on p. 12 makes sharpening gouges a lot easier and helps you reproduce an edge accurately time after

SHARPENING A GOUGE. Begin by raising the tool handle to pivot the bevel onto the grinding wheel (top). Then grind the wings by pushing the tool up the wheel as you roll it first to one side, then the other (above).

GRINDING JIG. Although not foolproof, a jig like this makes it easy to sharpen gouges with a consistent bevel time after time.

time. A good edge isn't guaranteed even with a jig, though. You can still mess it up if you don't keep the tool moving and rolling as you move it across the wheel.

Setting Up the Lathe

I usually work on my Vicmarc VL300, a full-size lathe that has a swing-sway tailstock support. It's the lathe you'll see for the larger pieces in this book. Otherwise, you'll see the Vicmarc VL150, a mini-lathe on steroids with a 11¾-in (300mm) swing and 13¾ in. (350mm) between centers.

When you're working at the lathe, personal comfort is paramount. You don't want to have to bend over to see what you're doing, nor do you want hunched shoulders because the lathe is too high when you reach over the tool rest. Set up the lathe so its center height is at about your elbow height (see the bottom photo on p. 26).

You can make fine adjustments by standing on a mat or platform. If your shop has a concrete floor, a thick rubber mat relieves the hardness of the concrete.

TAMING VIBRATION AND DUST

Vibration is the enemy of turning, and a slightly out-of-balance block of wood spinning at too high a speed can cause even a heavy lathe to jump around—literally. A vibrating lathe makes fine tool control impossible and turning dangerous. Consequently, lathes cannot be too heavy or anchored firmly enough. (My large Vicmarc, which weighs close to 700 lb., or 300kg, rarely needs to be bolted down, but it is.) My smaller lathe weighs about 136 lb. (62kg) and is my traveling lathe. It's not bolted to the floor, but rests on a stout base weighted with wood waiting to be turned. Pig-iron ingots or concrete blocks would be better still.

Dust extraction is a major expense, but worth it for the health of your lungs and to maintain a dust-free workspace. The headstock of my larger lathe is surrounded by dust-extraction intakes that collect all the fine dust and remove it from the workshop. The shelf between the lathe bed and the wall also helps corral dust. Heavier shavings fill the dust-extractor bags too quickly, so I shovel them directly into bags at the end of each day.

THE TOOL REST

Most tool rests are made of steel that's soft enough to dent easily. Nicks and dents on a rest will catch a tool, so file the top regularly to smooth the surface. If your lathe has a flat-topped rest, it's worth grinding the back to an angle so the tool pivots on a thinner top. Better still, weld on a hardened steel bar that's less easily damaged. The most user-friendly rests are shaped with space for your hand beneath the tool, like the Robust rests I use. These are topped with a hardened rod and never need filing.

MINI-LATHE. A smaller lathe like my Vicmarc VL150 is more affordable, with a capacity that more than gratifies the needs of most turners.

Chucks

I began to turn wood in 1970, 15 years before any of the modern self-centering four-jaw wood-turning chucks were developed. Back then, turners used either knuckle-busting three-jaw engineer's chucks or cup chucks for which most blanks had to be turned to fit. We were very good at turning wooden chucks as needed, like the one on p. 93. If you're on a tight budget, you can still work that way and develop all manner of skills chuck owners don't have. However, modern mechanical chucks make holding wood a lot easier than it used to be.

Self-centering four-jaw chucks are now regarded as essential lathe accessories. You can manage with just one with a single set of standard jaws. You can buy additional jaw sets in different sizes as needed. Buying additional chuck bodies also makes sense, because it's tedious to change chuck jaws.

I used to think you couldn't have too many chucks. I know several hobbyist turners with more than 20, but I've leveled off at about 14. For most of the projects in this book you can use the 4 shown in the photo below.

What I want more than anything else on a chuck are dovetail jaws without a chamfered rim. That design enables you to grip a small tenon without damaging the wood. If a dovetail jaw has chamfered rims, like those shown on the facing page, you need a longer tenon for the jaws to get a grip. Even then, the jaws always damage the wood, so you can never take anything finished from the chuck. (Having said that, chuck marks will enhance some wheels.)

Smooth chuck jaws with a depth equal to their diameter are handy when turning spheres as well as for re-chucking all manner of other jobs.

ESSENTIAL CHUCKS. In the foreground is a Jacobs chuck, used in the tailstock when drilling holes, or in the head-stock for holding small spindles. At right is a dedicated screw chuck to use for faceplate turning. Next to the screw chuck is a small self-centering chuck with Shark jaws; they are especially good for holding blanks for sets of wheels and the like. In the background at left is a self-centering chuck with pin jaws, which hold small spindle blanks, drills, sanding disks, and such.

CHAMFERED CHUCK JAWS. The chamfered inner lip of these jaws prevents you from gripping very short tenons, and the serrations always damage the wood being gripped. Smooth jaws with unbroken rims are preferable.

Other Tools

ABRASIVES AND SANDERS

You will need abrasives to smooth your surfaces. If you choose your wood carefully and get a good finish off the tools, you might need only 180-grit and finer. Occasionally I start with 120-grit, but mostly I begin with 180-grit, working up to 400-grit. For these projects, however, I regard 240-grit as close to overkill, because most of these toys will suffer intense wear and tear.

The belt/disk sander, shown in the photo above right, is a tool I use daily for all manner of small jobs. It makes short work of rounding corners, sanding edges and sawn surfaces, and shaping and smoothing parts that are not turned.

A basic substitute is a sanding table that fits into the lathe bed, like the one shown in the photo at right. It has a hook-and-loop-backed sanding disk on a 6-in. (152mm) faceplate. You can also turn a disk to fit on a self-centering chuck or screw chuck.

SAWS

I can't imagine life without my bandsaw, which is in the background of the photo above right. Set up properly and with the right blades, a

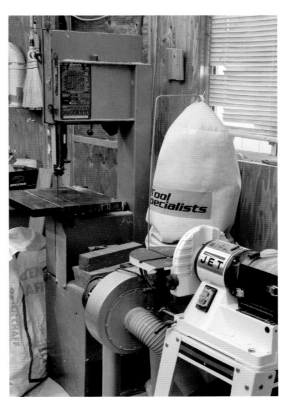

HANDY SANDER. Belt/disk sanders like this one come in many sizes and make it easy to shape and finish a wide range of pieces.

SHOPMADE SANDER. A lathe can easily double as a sander with abrasive attached to a faceplate or turned disk and a table that fits on the lathe bed.

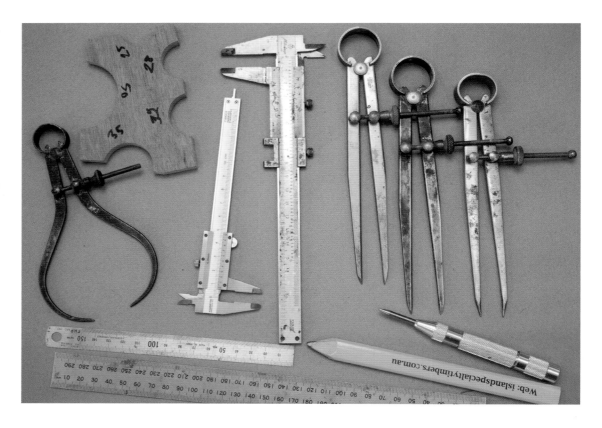

MADE TO MEASURE. Across the top, from left to right: spring calipers; a shopmade template for sizing beads; two vernier calipers, for measuring inside or outside diameters; spring dividers. Across the bottom are two rulers, a yellow pencil, and a spring punch for marking centers.

bandsaw is unsurpassed for cutting curves. The only downside is that you cannot begin a cut in the middle of a wide board: All cuts have to start on the edge because the blade is continuous. For many home woodworking shops, a 14-in. (356mm) bandsaw makes a good all-around choice. The size refers to the throat, or distance from the upper wheel support to the blade. Most 14-in. bandsaws can cut a block of wood up to 6 in. thick, but they can easily be modified to double that cutting capacity. When purchasing a bandsaw, I recommend favoring the depth of cut (the thickness you can cut), over the throat width.

If you need to start a cut in the middle of a board or saw very intricate curves, you need a scroll saw. Its finer blades mean the cut is narrower than on any bandsaw, and the curves can be much tighter. The downside is that a scroll saw works best in material less than 1 in. (25mm) thick, although some can cut twice that thickness. A tablesaw is useful for accurately cutting spindle blanks and squaring short boards.

MEASURING TOOLS

There's a lot of measuring involved in making sets of wheels or evenly graduated rings. You'll want to have several pairs of dividers and calipers along with a ruler or two. The photo above shows some essential measuring devices.

WOOD & PREPARING BLANKS

All wood needs to be dried before it becomes reasonably stable. Even then, wood can still shrink or swell slightly with changes in humidity. That's why doors jam in some seasons and not in others. Most of the components for the projects in this book need to be made from well-seasoned wood that is reasonably clear of loose knots and free of splits. This chapter gives you an overview of where to find wood and what to look for when selecting material for these projects. Finally, I offer some advice on grain alignment and preparing blanks for turning on the lathe.

RAW MATERIAL. There are many sources of good wood, some of it available absolutely free.

OLD BUT GOOD. You need not limit your choices to new wood. You can dismantle old furniture and recycle the pieces.

TREASURE FROM TRASH. It's a good idea to save offcuts and scraps like these. You never know when they may be useful.

Where to Find Wood

AT HOME CENTERS AND LUMBERYARDS

Pine, fir, or poplar from your local home center or lumberyard will be ideal for most of the projects in this book. These plain, pale woods are a bit dull to look at, but are ideal for things like peg dolls, where you don't want strong growth rings to impinge on your drawings. You can always stain them any color you like. The wood is also kiln-dried and thus well-seasoned.

This lumber is offered in a limited range of sizes, based on its thickness—nominally 1 in. or 2 in. thick, in widths from 2 in. to 12 in. (50mm to 300mm). If you are new to purchasing lumber, be prepared for the wood to be smaller than you might expect. A board called a 2×4 (or 2 in. thick by 4 in. wide) might actually measure 1½ in. by 3½ in. (38mm by 90mm). You pay for the waste, but you'll have nicely dimensioned material to work with. When you go shopping, take a tape measure to be sure you get the size you need. Check also that it's not twisted by looking along its length.

AT HARDWOOD DEALERS AND WOODWORKING RETAILERS

For higher quality and more decorative woods, try dedicated hardwood dealers or woodworking stores. The oak, maple, mahogany, cherry, and ash you are likely to find are well known for their stability and workability and unlikely to warp. Many of these sources also sell exotic tropical hardwoods. Most of the wood these retailers sell is kiln-dried, but rough rather than planed smooth.

IN RECYCLED FURNITURE

For wood that is well-seasoned and inexpensive, look for furniture in junk shops and thrift stores that can be knocked apart. A lot of basic furniture was constructed of good-quality softwood. The endgrain will reveal if it's real wood. It's probably covered in thick or chipped varnish or lacquer and looks pretty unpromising. But there can be treasure under the grime. For example, the stained and tenoned silky-oak board, center front in the top photo on the facing page, was formerly part of a drafting table. It is now reincarnated as wands like the one at left in the photo on p. 80.

IN THE SHOP

Professional woodworkers like me accumulate piles of offcuts that might be useful one day. The boxfuls shown on the facing page were always meant to be beads, wheels, and little wooden men. It's worth approaching anyone who works with real wood just to see what they might want to get rid of.

As a professional turner concentrating on bowls, I used to throw at least a ton of offcuts into the stove each year. But much of that wood could have been turned into small production items rather than heat. A major advantage of using up old, odd scraps is that they will be well-seasoned even if they weren't kiln-dried in the first place. Air-dried wood is much nicer to use for both workability and dust.

FROM ARBORISTS

Wherever there are trees, you can pick up logs and limbs from landscape services or arborists keen to avoid dumping them. You can convert green logs to seasoned boards easily enough if you have the equipment and space, but the wood needs time to season.

The old rule of thumb for drying wood is a year per inch (25mm) of thickness, plus a year. Remember, too, that wood shrinks in width but barely at all in length, and that as it dries it will usually warp and twist as the annular growth rings try to straighten themselves. This is why square-sectioned spindle blanks can go diamond shaped. When your wood is fully seasoned, further warping shouldn't be too much of a problem, although you can never guarantee that wood won't change with the humidity of different seasons.

STILL USEFUL. Although badly split, the casuarina log at left could still be cut to produce useful wood for a toy.

I failed to mill the casuarina and pistachio logs shown in the photo on p. 19 when they were green. Even so, I had enough material between the splits for a set of skittles.

What to Look For

The wood for most of these projects needs to be completely dry and therefore stable. Green (freshly cut) logs will shrink, warp, and split as they dry and take three years or more to do so. Although you might be able to cope with the odd split, you don't want the wood warping on you if it is meant to become a wheel axle that might jam. Never use unseasoned wood for any component that needs to remain stable. Where stability isn't an issue, as when making beads, a bit of grain collapse can add texture and character. Even then, it is prudent not to use wood within six months of its being cut, because it is too likely to split.

If you can score wood with your thumbnail, it's probably best avoided for being too soft and easily damaged by a marauding 2-year-old. For thin components, plywood is often a better option than solid wood. Be sure it's good quality, with edges that can be sanded smooth and not subject to splintering thereafter. You can test a finished piece by knocking it against a hard surface or even gnawing at it with a pair of pliers. If it copes with that, chances are a toddler's chewing won't achieve much. Finishing plywood with epoxy is another option that toughens the surface. Edges should be rounded.

Small kids love color, so if you're going to use stains, dyes, or paint, consider using drab woods like poplar, alder, or pine, which are inexpensive as well as easy to work and finish.

Short and less-than-perfect boards are usually less expensive than their larger, top-grade counterparts. Most of the components you'll be turning require small blanks, so it's possible to get

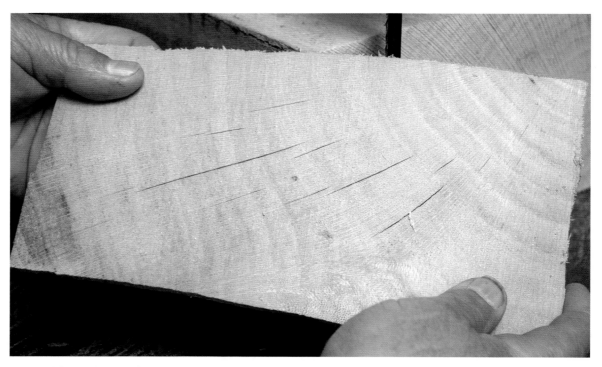

STRENGTH TEST. Bending a thin piece sawn from the end of a board will reveal any hidden splits that will weaken the wood.

really good value from these boards because you can cut around the defects.

Preparing Blanks

How the grain lies within a component is very important for the strength of that component. The sliver of endgrain shown in the photo on the facing page will break easily because the grain runs vertically between the two faces. A stick is difficult to break because the grain runs the length of the stick. That may seem blindingly obvious, but I frequently encounter woodworkers who seem to have forgotten this basic woodworking tenet. Anything long and stick-like needs to have the grain parallel to its longest sides, like the blanks shown above right. Disks for cross-grain or facework are cut from boards like those below right. Ideally, disks for facework should be flattened on one face so that the wood sits firmly against a screw chuck.

The roughest lump of wood is soon turned round on a lathe, so for completely round components like wands or wheels, nicely squared and planed blanks are not essential. However, you do want squared ends on spindle blanks held with a spur drive.

There is one exception, however. If you're making a project that incorporates holes for axles and people, it's best to drill those holes before you turn the blank. For accurate drilling, it's essential to begin with squared blanks that have parallel sides. I have a basic jointer/planer; with any blank more than a foot long, I joint it and then run it through the planer until both faces are smooth. I don't worry too much about retaining a random, or live, edge, but I do take thicknessed boards to my tablesaw or bandsaw and cut one side square to the parallel faces.

If you're turning toys, beads of some sort will come into your life. As you'll see in Chapter 7, bead blanks are drilled so they can be turned between cones. It helps to cut standard sizes to make drilling lots of blanks easier.

SPINDLE SUPPLY. These blanks are cut so the grain runs along their length. They're meant for axles, dowels, and the like.

FACEWORK SUPPLY. Disks for facework are cut from boards so the grain runs at right angles to the lathe axis. Cross-grained blanks should be mounted on a screw chuck or faceplate.

SHOP SAFETY BASICS

1 Use a push stick whenever your fingers will come within an inch of a saw blade. Whenever possible, keep your fingers behind a bandsaw blade. When cross-cutting a squared length, keep your fingers on top or to the right side of the wood, not on the blade side. I've learned the hard way that a bandsaw blade can grab a squared block and snap it over to pinch a finger between the block and the table. I had the end of one finger sewn back on, but the nerves remain damaged. After three years, the end of that finger remains numb.

2 Material for any woodworking project should be free of defects unless you can feature them. For instance, knotholes where the knot has fallen out present no immediate danger and might be used to represent a window. Splits should always be cut away.

3 When a block has a major split along the grain, cut it along the split and then decide what to do with the two parts. I was able to use the badly split casuarina log shown on p. 19 by cutting it up with an electric chainsaw. After cutting again along other splits, I went to the bandsaw to square up what was left. The log yielded the blanks for the "pigs" shown on p. 175.

WOOD RESCUE, STAGE ONE. To salvage a log plagued with splits, begin by cutting along them, here using a chainsaw.

WOOD RESCUE, STAGE TWO. Square up the pieces of log on the bandsaw and cut them roughly to the size you need.

WOOD, SALVAGED. By carefully working around the splits in the log, I managed to get some useful blanks.

4 A safe way to bandsaw a short length of a log is to stand it on end (photo below). The short boards can then be cut on their sides.

5 To check if endgrain is split, cut a thin slice off the end, then bend it as shown on p. 20. This will reveal any cracks that aren't immediately apparent.

SAFE BANDSAWING. To cut a short log on the bandsaw, stand it on end for stability. Note, too, that my right hand is away from the blade, and that I'm moving the wood into the cut by using a push stick in my left hand.

4 THINGS WE FORGET (BUT SHOULDN'T)

Most readers of this book will probably have some turning experience. I know that many will have learned to turn using my earlier books and videos. The more we turn, the better we get—for the most part. But the more we turn, the easier it is to fall into some bad habits. Recently, I watched a couple of dozen well-known turners in action, some who rely on the craft for a living. Astonishingly (to me at least), many were turning contrary to, or unaware of, many of the craft's best practices, and rarely to any advantage I could discern. We can all become lackadaisical and occasionally forget some absolute basics, so here are a few reminders.

Safety

Wear a face shield or visor. It protects your face and eyes from wood chips and sparks from grinders.

Never leave machines running unattended. This is especially important with regard to saws and when you have wood mounted on the lathe. A dust extractor is an exception.

Always have your hand on a key or lever in a chuck. Never leave a key in a chuck unattended.

If you start a lathe or drill press with a key in the chuck, it can fly in any direction.

Wear earmuffs or earplugs to preserve your hearing. I can guarantee that you don't want tinnitus if you can avoid it, so always use ear protection when using power saws and planers. While lathes are quiet, some turning isn't. If the sound becomes too penetrating as you turn, it's sensible to use earplugs.

Install and use good dust collection. This is especially important when you are sanding. Fine dust will find its way deep into your lungs, where it can eventually cause grave health problems. You need to wear a mask or, better still, an impact-resistant helmet with built-in dust protection. When sanding, have dust-extractor intakes in front of and behind the headstock, like the setup on my VL150 lathe (see the photo on the facing page).

Always check the speed before starting the lathe. If your lathe has variable speed control, develop the habit of turning it back to zero then up very slightly, so you always start at a slow, safe speed. Most variable-speed lathes also have the drive belt mounted on pulleys, creating two or three speed ranges; position the belt to limit the maximum speed. The lower the speed range, the more control you have over the precise speed.

Never try to turn wood that is vibrating as it spins. As a safety measure, my lathes are set to run at a maximum speed of 2,000 rpm. I have no need for higher speeds, even for very thin spindles.

Never stand in line with the work when you start a lathe. This is particularly important when the project is held using only a faceplate or chuck with no tailstock support. If the speed is too fast, you won't have time to evade the wood as it flies off the lathe. Sometimes, wood just flies apart.

Remember that sharp rims cut deep. It's very easy to create razor-sharp edges as you turn, particularly on facework rims. If your hand slips onto one, it will slice you to the bone in an instant. Get into the habit of softening edges with a scrap of 100-grit or 120-grit abrasive, or use a gouge on its side.

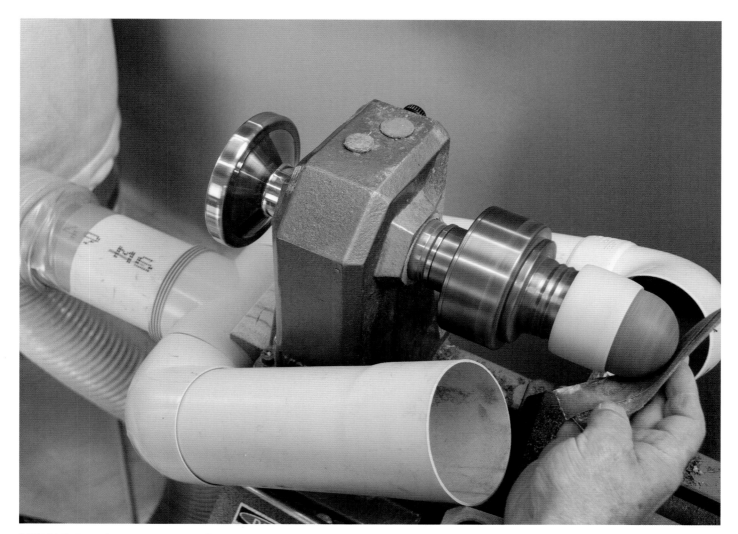

REMOVE DANGEROUS DUST. When sanding, rig a dust extractor to collect the fine dust. On this setup of mine, the pipes leading from the T-junction occasionally get in the way, but I can easily replace them with shorter sections.

IDEAL CUTTING ANGLE. Hold a skew chisel or gouge so that the part of the edge that is cutting is at about 45 degrees to the on-coming wood.

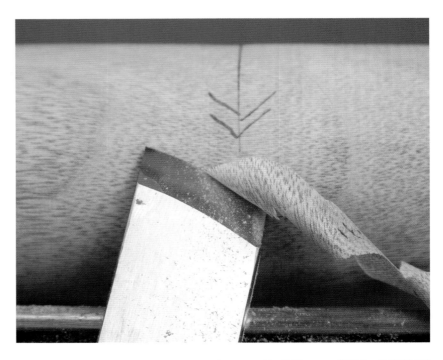

GOOD WORKING STANCE. Hold the tool near the ferrule to avoid cramping your arm and keep the handle in close to your body. Use your whole body, not just your arms, to move the tool.

Turning Basics

Let the wood come to the tool. Let the lathe do the work. All you have to do is hold a tool so that wood is sheared off as it passes over the tool's edge.

Keep the portion of the edge that is cutting at about 45 degrees to the wood. This applies mainly to skew chisels and gouges, tools designed to slice wood cleanly when the bevel rubs the wood (top photo, facing page). You don't need to push the tool hard against the wood, but you do need to hold it firmly on the rest.

Move with the tool. Keep your feet shoulder-width apart and keep the tool handle in at your side. Use your whole body, not just your arms, to move the tool (bottom photo, facing page). Sway with the tool handle from your knees. If you keep your hand on the handle near the ferrule rather than the end of the handle, your hand will move less and you'll be less cramped physically.

There is no "correct height" for the tool rest. The precise height of the rest depends on which tool you are using for what job and on your height in relation to center. (Ideally, the lathe's center height should be about the height of your elbow.) On a large-diameter spindle, the rest might need to be high so you can stand comfortably with a skew chisel or gouge handle dropped slightly below horizontal. When you part off the same spindle, the rest needs to be lower so you don't have to stand on tiptoe to reach over the rest. If you are hollowing endgrain with a scraper, the rest needs to be at or even a little above the center.

Keep tools sharp. This sounds so basic and so obvious, but one of the most difficult things to learn is when a sharp tool could be sharper. If it even vaguely crosses your mind that a tool might need sharpening, go straight to the grinder and do it. As with turning, don't push the tool into the grinding wheel. Let the wheel come to the tool. Just hold the tool firmly on the rest, with the bevel resting lightly on the wheel.

Professional turners sharpen freehand for speed, and it's a nice skill to have, but jigs make sharpening much easier and help you maintain the shape of the cutting edge. Jigs are not a panacea, however. You can still mess up an edge. You need to keep the tool moving on the grinding wheel to avoid creating flat sections and dips (see pp. 10–11).

Cut more slowly as the tool moves toward the center. Wood moves more slowly near center, so you need to slow the rate at which you move the tool into the cut. If you push the tool into the wood at the same speed all the way to center, you'll tear the grain, especially on the endgrain of spindlework.

Listen to the lathe. Stop the lathe and ascertain the cause or origin of any sound you don't recognize. Hollow sounds indicate splits or loose bark, for instance. A shriek as you turn on the lathe usually means the spindle is locked and the belt is slipping. It wears the belt but is no big deal and not dangerous.

Never use scrapers for spindle turning. That will leave you with a lot of sanding. Scrapers on spindles never do a good job unless the wood is really hard; even then, cutting tools are far superior.

Abrasives do not become finer with use. 120-grit abrasive does not become 180-grit with use, then 220-grit, and so on. When abrasive stops cutting, throw it away and get a fresh piece. Fold abrasives in three, so the cutting surface sits against backing. Fold cloth-backed abrasive with the warp—usually along the lettering.

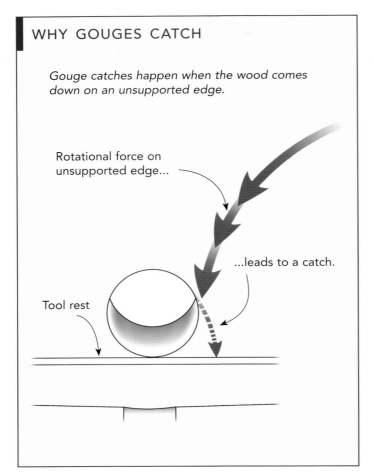

WHY GOUGES CATCH

Gouge catches happen when the wood comes down on an unsupported edge.

Rotational force on unsupported edge...

...leads to a catch.

Tool rest

STARTING A CUT WITH A GOUGE. With a spindle or detail gouge, roll the tool on its side so the cutting edge is supported. Spindle roughing gouges can be started flute-up.

Tool Catches (and How to Avoid Them)

Unsupported edges catch. The portion of the edge that's cutting needs to be in line with the fulcrum, where the tool contacts the rest.

Remember the 1-2-3 rule. The simplest catch occurs if you let the tool edge contact the spinning wood before you put the tool on the rest. The wood instantly snaps the tool down onto the rest with a loud bang. To avoid that, follow these three steps: One, tool on rest; two, bevel on wood; three, lift the handle to arc the edge into the cut.

On endgrain, always start a gouge on its side. Gouge catches happen when the wood exerts pressure on an unsupported edge, as shown in the drawing above. So never start spindle or bowl gouges with the flute up.

Tilt a scraper down to avoid a catch. Scrapers catch when the angle between the top of the edge and the surface being cut is more than 90 degrees. Make sure you tilt a scraper down when cutting flat surfaces. Scrapers can tilt up on internal curves, but not on endgrain.

SKEW CATCH. To avoid a catch like the one shown above, be sure only the side of the bevel—not the edge—touches the work, as shown at right.

Skews catch when you let the edge roll back to contact what you just cut. To avoid skew-chisel catches when turning beads (like the fine example shown above) or on endgrain, only the bevel side should be against the wood (not the bevel face). Remember, too, that skew-chisel catches only mess up the wood: Gouge catches on face-work like bowls are much more dangerous.

5 TURNING CYLINDERS & DOWELS

Many of the projects in this book are based on cylinders turned between centers—the basic shape of wheels, skittles, peg men and women, and wheel axles. Turning square spindle blanks to round can be a tedious business when you're in the middle of a project, so it's handy to have cylinders roughed down and ready to go.

If you are relatively new to turning wood or out of practice, then schedule a session of cylinder-roughing for a good dose of one technique and to get you into a rhythm. You also get lots of gouge and skew-chisel practice when it doesn't matter if you have the odd catch. If you are right on top of the techniques, then you get a tedious job out of the way in one session. Either way, you can enjoy the shavings as you refine your techniques.

Roughing cylinders between centers might seem pretty basic and easy, but I've seen a lot of decent material wasted by turners who should have known better. It's easy to mess up a blank if you don't approach it the right way, so here's how to go about it.

Lathe Setup and Speeds

It's best to mount spindle blanks more than 1 in. (25mm) square between centers, so you can turn the whole blank in one go. For thinner blanks, hold one end in a chuck and support the other end with the tailstock. Whenever possible, keep the blanks slightly shorter than the tool rest so you don't have to move it frequently. Blanks held in a chuck should project no more than 8 in. (200mm); catches at the end of a blank any longer than that are dangerous, usually pulling the blank from the jaws. To locate the centers of the blanks, draw diagonals on the ends, as seen on some of the blanks in the photo on the facing page. Or do as I do and mount them by eye. The more you do stuff by eye, the better you become. It's always satisfying to get it right.

When setting lathe speeds, err on the side of caution. Early in my turning career, while turning a small scoop at 2,250 rpm, I was asked to make a lamp base from a piece of teak 6 in. (150mm) square and 14 in. (355mm) long. I forgot to lower the speed, so when I restarted the lathe, that large, heavy lump of teak flew off and hit me on the forehead. It left a huge purple bump, but if my head had been up I'd have lost all my front teeth. (I didn't wear a face shield in those days, which didn't help.) Large-diameter blanks should always be started at low speeds; that lamp base should have been started at about 700 rpm.

Get into the habit of starting variable-speed lathes at a low speed as a matter of course. The chart on the facing page indicates maximum

X MARKS THE CENTER. Connect the corners of a square blank to find the center for accurate mounting on the lathe.

speeds, but it is always prudent to rough squares to round at slightly lower speeds.

Stage One: Square to Round

Never start roughing at the midpoint of a spindle blank. If the grain is twisted, you can lose a lot more wood than you want as lengths splinter away. Those big splinters can be dangerous.

For the initial roughing cuts, make a series of scooping cuts, starting at one end and working steadily back to the other, as shown in the top left photo on p. 32. Roll the gouge in the direction of the cut and keep the gouge square to the blank as you raise the handle to pivot the edge into the cut.

When you're turning a spindle, it helps to have a hollowed tool rest you can use as a guide. By using an underhand grip (see the top right photo on p. 32), you can keep your forefinger in the cove beneath the top of the rest. If you use an overhand grip (see the center left photo on p. 32), keep the side of your hand in the cove. With either grip, you can keep the tool in a fixed

DIAMETER	LENGTH	
	6 in. (150mm)	12 in. (300mm)
⅜ in. (10mm)	2,500 rpm	2,000 rpm
1 in. (25mm)	2,250 rpm	2,000 rpm
2 in. (51mm)	2,000 rpm	1,750 rpm
3 in. (76mm)	1,750 rpm	1,250 rpm
4 in. (100mm)	1,250 rpm	1,000 rpm
5 in. (125mm)	1,000 rpm	900 rpm
6 in. (150mm)	900 rpm	800 rpm

MAXIMUM LATHE SPEEDS FOR EVEN-GRAINED BLANKS BETWEEN CENTERS

For safety's sake, blanks held in a chuck, or that are unevenly balanced with a combination of heavy heartwood and lighter-weight sapwood, should be started at half these speeds.

FIRST STAGE OF ROUGHING. Working back from one end of the blank, make a series of scooping cuts to begin taking it from square to round.

UNDERHAND GRIP. If you use a concave tool rest, you can position your index finger in the recess to guide the gouge along the blank. This helps keep the cuts uniform.

OVERHAND GRIP. If you wrap your fingers over the gouge, keep the heel of your hand in the tool rest's recess to guide the tool evenly along the blank.

ALTERNATIVE GOUGE. A shallow roughing gouge like this one works well for turning large blanks round.

SLOW BUT EFFECTIVE. A ½-in. (13mm) spindle gouge can also be used for roughing, but the tool's small size makes the work go slowly.

position relative to the cut and the tool rest, so it becomes a jig for your hand as the cut proceeds.

The deep-fluted roughing gouges shown here are designed for cutting close to a tool rest and are intended strictly for roughing spindles: They should *never* be used for roughing bowls. Spindle roughing gouges are used primarily for peeling cuts, with the tool rolled on its side. The bevel does not rub the wood and the portion of the edge doing the cutting lies parallel to the lathe axis. Note also that the blade doesn't point at center along the radius—that would be a

scraping cut—but slightly above center, with the handle a few degrees below horizontal.

For roughing blanks more than 2⅜ in. (60mm) square, I prefer a 1-in. (25mm) shallow roughing gouge, like the one shown in the center right photo on the facing page. But you can also use a standard ½-in. (13mm) spindle gouge, as shown in the bottom photo on the facing page, although the smaller gouge will take a bit longer to do the roughing. The bottom line is that you can rough down even a large spindle blank with almost any gouge. When you've turned the square nearly round, use the gouge to make rapid passes the entire length of the blank in one pass, leaving a spiral groove, as shown above.

For smaller blanks, I find it more convenient to use a skew chisel for both roughing and smoothing (see photo at right).

Stage Two: Square the Endgrain

Whenever you rough down or turn a cylinder or blank, be sure to square each end so that when you mount the blank in a chuck it will seat square in the jaws. Each end should be flat to slightly concave, never domed. A peeling cut

SQUARING THE HEADSTOCK END. Use a skew chisel held flat on the tool rest to square the end. To remove the nub at the center, remount the blank in a chuck and turn it away.

SQUARING THE TAILSTOCK END. You can square the end of a blank right up to the revolving center by using a spindle gouge rolled on its side.

with the tool flat on the rest removes the waste quickly, as shown in the top photo at left, but the best surface comes when you ease the bevel side into the endgrain, moving the tool along the rest rather than toward the center. This is the easiest way to clean up the headstock end of the blank, where the possibility of hitting the spur center is always a concern. To remove the nub at the drive end, grab the other end in a chuck and turn it away.

At the tailstock end, you can get a very clean cut from a ½-in. (13mm) spindle gouge, as shown in the bottom left photo. Start the cut with the gouge on its side and roll it very slightly counter-clockwise once the bevel is rubbing against the wood. It helps to have the tool rest at an angle. Cut right to the cone on the revolving center, rolling the gouge right on its side at the end of the cut. Often you need to tighten the tail center very slightly to take up some slack. This will leave the endgrain flat with a small hole at the center, but no nub to remove.

Stage Three: True the Cylinder to Size

When you need a cylinder with a precise diameter, set calipers to the required dimension and establish it at regular intervals along the blank. Use the calipers in conjunction with a parting tool, as shown on the facing page. Rigid Vernier calipers can be pushed over the work, provided the jaw tips are rounded and smooth, which you will have to do on a sander. The springy balloon calipers must be pulled rather than pushed over the blank. If you push them over a spindle they will catch, probably spring open, and certainly be permanently bent, as were these in 1970. As you start the parting cut, rest the jaws in the groove and pull gently until the jaws slide free. Be sure that *both* jaws are in the groove, though, otherwise you'll get a much smaller diameter than you want.

Production spindle-turners occasionally convert an open-end wrench to a sizing tool, like the

SETTING A DIAMETER. You can use either Vernier calipers (left) or balloon callipers (below left) in conjunction with a parting tool to establish a uniform series of diameters along a blank. Then turn away the waste between them.

FIXED SIZE. An open-end wrench with the top jaw sharpened like a parting tool makes a good gauge for sizing a spindle.

PLANE AWAY. Use a skew chisel to slice away the wood between the set diameters, leaving a smooth cylinder that will need very little sanding.

AVOIDING TEAROUT. Areas of cross or twisted grain are prone to tearout. To avoid that, make a series of light peeling cuts with the skew held so its edge is tilted slightly above horizontal.

one shown in the top photo at left, sharpening the upper jaw by grinding the top so it cuts like a parting tool. If you can slide the wrench along the cylinder without twisting it, you have sized the cylinder. The main advantage of using a wrench is that the jaws are fixed, whereas calipers can change.

Use a skew chisel to plane away the surplus down to your set diameters (see the center photo at left). For a slicing cut, keep the bevel on the wood and position the edge at an angle to the oncoming wood so you get decent curly shavings. If you end up with cleanly cut ridges, the bevel is not rubbing the wood. If you produce spiral chatter marks, you are pushing the tool too hard against the wood.

Areas of cross or twisted grain can often tear out on a cylinder. A good way to clean this up, or ensure it doesn't happen in the first place, is to use a skew chisel with a slightly radiused edge for a low peeling cut, as shown in the bottom left photo. For this cut, keep the tool flat on the rest with the handle dropped slightly below horizontal. Move the tool back and forth along the rest so that the edge barely strokes the wood, removing only the sort of dust and very small shavings you see in the middle of the edge. A peeling cut doesn't leave the surface quite as smooth as a shear cut, but there is no risk of tearout.

If you are sanding now, use a sanding block or short length of flat wood to back the abrasive. This helps you maintain an even diameter while eliminating small bumps.

Turning Thin Dowels

Many of the toy projects require short lengths of cylindrical rod or dowel for wheel axles or posts. You could buy ready-made dowels, but turning short, thin pieces gives you wonderful tool practice. It's very satisfying when you cut the wood so cleanly it doesn't need sanding. Axles are usually hidden in these toys, so you can even accommodate a few decorative spirals, chatter marks, and small catches.

HOLDING A THIN BLANK. This shows the simplest method: Drive one end of the blank into the headstock spindle and use a revolving center in the tailstock to support the other end

HOW TO HOLD THIN BLANKS

When turning anything long and thin, life is much easier if you grip the drive end in a chuck or pound one end straight into the headstock's Morse taper (as shown above), rather than mount the blank between centers. The idea is to hold the blank at one end and *support* it at the other with minimal pressure from a revolving center in the tailstock. To achieve this, secure the blank at the headstock and move the live center close to, but not in, the wood. When you have the blank centered, advance the tailstock so that the revolving center supports the blank without bending it. If you drive the blank into the Morse taper, use glancing blows on the end-grain to center the wood before advancing the tailstock.

If you hold the blank with a drill chuck, it helps to round the end of the blank, either with a pocketknife or skew chisel (because you're a turner with a sharp skew) or by twirling the end against a sander. When you tighten a drill chuck, its jaws move forward, pushing the blank toward and onto the live center. If that doesn't bend the blank, the pressure will probably split it, so you need to retract the tailstock as you tighten the chuck.

Never mount long thin blanks between conical centers: The pressure needed to spin the wood will bend the blank if the cones don't split it first. Both scenarios are worth avoiding.

TURNING TECHNIQUE

All you need to turn small-diameter blanks is a ¾-in. (19mm) skew chisel. As with roughing any cylinder, work from one end to the other. Never start in the middle, because you risk having the corners splinter away.

If you're holding one end of the blank with a chuck or in the spindle, begin by making a V-groove with the long point of the skew chisel. This allows you to make a clean cut against the chuck or spindle (see the photo below).

Use the long point of the skew to make a series of planing cuts from right to left that remove the square shoulders (see the top photo on p. 38).

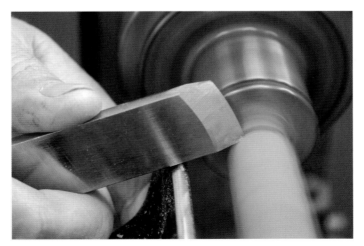

CLEAN SHOULDER. Make a V-cut with the long point of a skew chisel to keep the ends of a thin spindle clean.

The shavings are messy, but they break away cleanly at the groove. After that, use the edge to make conventional shearing cuts, taking a series of scoops to remove the square corners.

As a blank becomes thinner, you'll have to equalize any tool pressure against the wood using your hand. Working back from the drive, you'll initially use your palm to hold the tool on the rest and wrap your fingers around the wood, as shown in the bottom photo on p. 33. Once there is space between the tool and the drive for your hand, it's best to curl your fingers around the spindle and control the skew with your

PLANE OFF THE SHOULDERS. Use a skew chisel's long point to remove the corners of the blank to the V-cut. The rough shavings will come away cleanly.

HUMAN STEADY REST. Use your fingers to support a thin spindle so that it doesn't flex. Your thumb guides the skew chisel.

thumb, as shown in the bottom photo on the facing page. As you cut toward the tailstock, use the skew long-point-up so you can cut toward and off the end of the blank (see the photo at right). Remember, you're trying to let the wood come to the tool; you don't need to push the edge hard against the wood.

When the blank is nearly round, use calipers to set a series of diameters along the length of the blank (see p. 35). Then take planing cuts, as shown below. Use the skew long-point-down to work down to those diameters.

NEARING THE END. Use the skew long-point-up when you cut near the tailstock end of the spindle.

PLANE TO SIZE. A series of planing cuts, with the skew held long-point-down, will take a thin spindle down to size.

6 TURNING WHEELS

Whenever I've asked people who have young children which toys are the favorite, the answer is almost invariably, "Anything with wheels." That must be why, traditionally,

many toys have wheels. The moment a child is crawling and able to free one hand, chances are that hand will grab something with wheels.

No commercial toymaker will turn wheels or beads by hand when an automatic lathe can pop

GET ROLLING.
Toys with wheels are always popular. The details you add to the wheels you turn ensure that the toys will be unique and special.

The neatest option is the stopped axle (A), which passes through the body of the toy and fits into stopped holes in the wheels. Nearly as good is the through axle (B), although the ends must be sanded flush with the wheels. The pin axle (C) has less strength and requires more work at the lathe, turning the two short axles with hubs.

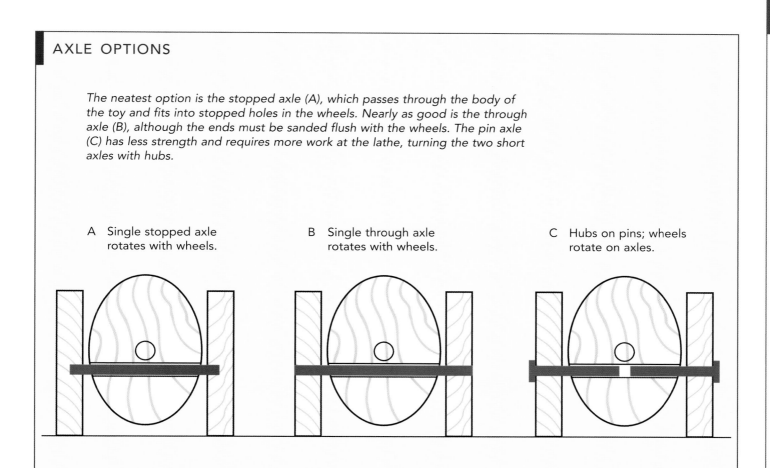

A Single stopped axle rotates with wheels.

B Single through axle rotates with wheels.

C Hubs on pins; wheels rotate on axles.

out 40 or more a minute, and they can be purchased in bulk for next to nothing per unit. However, such wheels are rarely as well finished as those you can turn yourself. And they will all be exactly the same, whereas yours can vary in size and be individually styled with matching hubs and other detail. And that's before you add color.

Wheels less than 3 in. (75mm) in diameter are generally made using endgrain, wood with the grain parallel to the lathe axis. It is easier to work this way, and the wood wears more evenly than does cross-grain. You can make a set of wheels from a single blank held in a chuck, so it's easier to make them exactly the same diameter. Wheels with the grain running across the

face have to be cut out and turned individually, so making sets the same diameter becomes much more difficult.

Wheel Design

How you attach a wheel to its axle affects how it looks and how you go about making it. Wheels can either be fixed to an axle or rotate on an axle. The drawing above shows three options for mounting a pair of wheels. As usual, there are benefits and disadvantages with each.

My preference is for a one-piece axle with wheels fixed to it, as shown at A and B in the drawing. Option A shows an enclosed axle, which I think is the neatest solution. The wheel is easy enough to make using a chuck with dovetail jaws, provided you can drill the stopped hole for the axle precisely at center. The major advantage of this wheel design is that it's easy to detail each face. The protruding axle (option B) has to be detailed or sanded flat to the wheel face. If the rim of the hole chips, as it can with cross-grain wheels, the hub will look messy. Option C is a pin axle. It looks good when it contrasts with the wheel, but it's not as strong as an axle connecting both wheels.

How to Turn Enclosed-Axle Wheels

This type of wheel is made in two stages. First, turn either a short tenon or a groove to fit your chuck jaws, then use it to hold the blank while you complete the other side.

If either the tenon or wheel diameter is exactly the same diameter as the chuck jaws, the jaws won't mark the wood. But even if they do, it's no big deal in this case—those marks are adding tread to each wheel, and the same on each one. It's a lot easier than carving. Here, chuck marks are an asset. You might even want to reverse or rotate each wheel in the chuck for more tread marks.

1 Turn a cylinder between centers. Make it the diameter of your wheels and long enough for the set you're turning. (For recommended lathe speeds, see p. 31.) Calculate the length you need by adding the size of the four elements shown in the chart above (the specific measurements are just examples).

So, in this example, four wheels require about 4¾ in. (120mm) of wood protruding from the chuck, some of which is spare and there in case you have a catch. Thicker wheels require a longer cylinder, of course. But don't work with a blank more than 8 in. (200mm) long in a chuck unsupported by the tail center.

CYLINDER LENGTH FOR ENCLOSED-AXLE WHEELS		
4 wheels ¾ in. (19mm) each	3 in.	76mm
3 parting cuts ¼ in. (6mm) each	¾ in.	18mm
1 spare wheel	1 in.	25mm
Allowance for tenon or groove for chuck jaws	1 in.	25mm
Total	**5¾ in.**	**144mm**

A heavy catch can be dangerous, pulling the blank out of the chuck. It's safer to turn one pair of wheels out of a short blank, rather than two pairs out of a longer one.

2 Mount the cylinder in your chuck, supporting the other end with the tail center for accuracy. Keep the tail center in place while you true the cylinder, as shown below. Do this even if the cylinder seems to run true. You want it spot on, otherwise any detail you put on the sides won't be concentric with the rim.

TRUING THE WHEEL BLANK. Use calipers to ensure a uniform diameter. Take very light peeling cuts with a skew chisel.

TRUE THE END. A skew chisel, long-point-down, leaves a smooth surface on the end of the wheel blank.

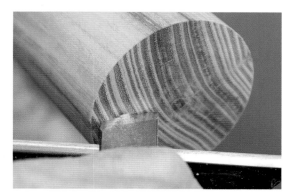

SMOOTH. A very light scraping cut with a skew will yield the smoothest endgrain.

3 True the endgrain. For safety and in case you have a catch, remove most of the waste before backing off the tailstock. Clean up the endgrain either with a skew chisel long-point-down, as shown in the top left photo, or with a spindle gouge (see the photo on p. 28). The gouge is less likely to catch, but the skew leaves a much better surface; just be sure you use the point with *only* the bevel *side* rubbing the end grain. A very gentle scraping cut that removes only dust will usually leave the finest surface off the tool, as shown in the photo above.

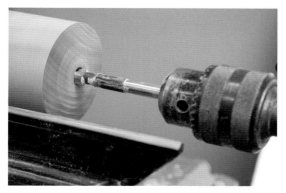

AXLE HOLE. Drill a hole nearly as deep as a wheel is wide. Wrap tape around the drill bit to gauge the depth.

4 Drill the stopped hole for the axle, as shown above. This wheel will be ¾ in. (19mm) wide, so I bore in ⅝ in. (16mm), using the blue tape wrapped around the drill as a guide. It helps to have a small dimple at the center to start the drill. Either bring up the tail center and advance its point into the wood, or make the dimple with the long point of a skew with the tool flat on its side on the rest.

5 Turn a detail that will also allow you to reverse-chuck the wheel. Cut a tenon as short as your chuck jaws will allow. (My Vicmarc chucks can grip a tenon as small as ¹⁄₃₂ in. [1.5mm], but yours may need to be longer.) You'll hold the wheel by this tenon so you can complete the outside. You can use a ruler and pencil to lay out the diameter, but dividers are more accurate. They also score the wood so you have a well-defined line to work to (see the photo below). The circle you score with the left

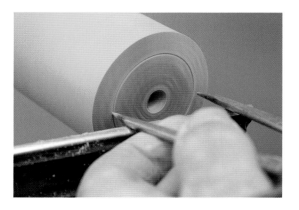

MARK A TENON FOR THE CHUCK. The circle you score with the left point needs to line up with the right point, but don't let the right point touch the wood.

point needs to line up with the right point, but don't let the right point touch the wood.

Use a skew chisel flat on the rest to create the tenon. Squeeze the bevel side gently into the endgrain to get a wispy ribbon of a shaving like the one shown in the top photo below. The cut should leave smooth endgrain that barely needs sanding.

If you want your wheels to have smooth sides, omit the tenon and have the jaws close around the rim. There is one drawback to this alternative, though: It's difficult to get a wheel running true unless it's wide enough to sit right into the chuck and proud of the chuck jaws. The trick is to turn one or two small V-grooves to locate the jaws, as shown in the bottom photo below. The grooves look like those on real car tires. Use the skew chisel's long point to make little arcing cuts to shape the grooves.

MAKE A TENON. Use the bevel side of a skew chisel to make a series of light cuts as you create the tenon.

V-GROOVE ALTERNATIVE. In lieu of cutting a tenon on the side of the wheel, you can cut shallow V-grooves in the rim. These allow a scroll chuck to grip the outside of the wheel accurately.

SAND AND POLISH. My typical finish is in the rag: beeswax thinned with a modicum of boiled linseed oil.

6 Sand and polish the endgrain and the grooved rim (see the photos above). If you plan to color the wheels with marker pens, now is a good time. If kids are involved with making the wheels, get them working now—they love to color spinning wood, and you have a chance to teach them some hand skills.

7 Lay out the wheel width with dividers, as shown in the top left photo on the facing page. Remove the wheel with a parting tool, as shown in the top right photo on the facing page. Cut straight in about 1/32 in. (1.5mm) to the left of the line you scored with the dividers. This allows for some torn endgrain that you'll turn away as you work to the line defining the width of the wheel. Once you have removed the first wheel, repeat steps 3 through 7 to make the rest, one at a time.

PART OFF THE WHEEL. Use a thin parting tool to separate the wheel from the blank. Cut to the left of the line scribed with dividers, to allow for torn endgrain and burnish marks that will need turning away.

MARK THE WIDTH. Grab the dividers again to establish the width of the wheel.

8 Remount the wheel to complete the other side. With the wheel settled in the chuck, turn away the waste, working back to the scored line, using a skew chisel long-point-down, as shown at right. As the photo shows, I'm shaping the outside of that wheel with a slight dome. On the other wheel, held by the tenon, I'm adding detail by using the skew flat on the rest as a scraper (photo, bottom right). I use the width of the skew chisel to locate and mark the diameter of the detail, measuring in from the rim of the wheel. There's no need to reach for a ruler when you can use what's in your hand.

9 Sand and polish the second face.
A final note. You can leave the tenon on one face of the wheel, or turn it away and make both faces match. If you choose the second option, you'll have to sandwich the wheel between the chuck and the tailstock (see the top left photo on p. 46).

REMOUNT AND TURN. Hold the wheel in a scroll chuck, either gripping the tenon or clamping around the rim (shown). Then begin shaping the face.

ADD DETAILS. Use a skew as a scraper to add grooves and other embellishments. You can use the tool's width to locate and mark these details.

SETUP FOR RE-TURNING. If you want to get rid of the tenon, reverse the wheel and hold it between the chuck and the tailstock. The tail center fits in the axle hole to ensure that the wheel runs true. The non-slip cloth between wheel and chuck affords both a grip and protection for the wood.

How to Turn Wheels between Cones

If you want absolutely plain wheels or don't have a suitable chuck, you can mount a blank with a hole through the center between a solid drive cone in the headstock and a revolving conical tail center, as shown at right. The tail center needs to press the wood firmly against the drive cone. Solid conical centers used to be supplied with every new lathe, but revolving centers are now more common. If you don't own a drive cone and can't find one commercially, you can easily turn one from hardwood. My cone centers come from Axminster Tool Centre, in England.

If you're nervous about spiral catches messing up the wood, forget them. They can't happen with this technique. If the tool catches or you push too hard into the cut, the wood will merely slip against the drive center, so you'll need to tighten the tailstock. The drive cone will leave a burnished ring, but you can hide that if you

wish by putting that side of the wheel on the inside. Working between cones is a particularly good way to refine your turning technique, because it helps you develop a lightness of touch. As always, think of letting the wood come to the tool and having the bevel resting on the wood, rather than pushed against it.

The main benefit of working between cones is that you can see the whole wheel as you are turning. And if you need to adjust the diameter of a wheel or add detail well after it was originally made, just pop it back on the lathe.

HOLDING WITHOUT A CHUCK. For wheels with a through-axle, drill a hole through the center of the blank. A solid cone center in the headstock drives the blank, while a revolving center in the tailstock pushes the blank against the drive.

SQUARE TO ROUND. To make the wheel blank round, take peeling cuts with a skew chisel.

TWO WAYS TO SQUARE THE FACES. You can either use the long point of a skew or a detail gouge (as shown) to square the faces of the wheel. With either tool, you can work right up to the conical center.

1 To turn the square to round, you can use a standard ½-in. (13mm) spindle gouge, but I prefer to use a skew chisel in peeling mode, as shown above. Keep the tool flat on the rest and slowly raise the tool handle to bring the blank to round. When the blank is round, use calipers to size the wheel.

2 Clean up the sides using a skew chisel's long point or a spindle or detail gouge, as shown above right. Or, you can use the skew chisel bevel side, as shown on p. 44. The detail gouge shown at right is a heavier and stronger version of a spindle gouge, but with a shallower flute. It lets you cut right to the cone, but each time you do so you'll need to tighten the tailstock very slightly to take up the slack. If you find one side much more difficult to turn than the other, simply reverse the wheel between the cones so you're always making the same cut.

3 If you want a rounded wheel, make a pencil mark on the middle of the blank, then remove the corners with a spindle gouge, working away from the mark, as shown in the bottom right photo.

If you're making a pair or set of wheels and don't trust your eye to get the roundovers uniform, use a template like the one shown in

MARK AND ROLL. Make a pencil line at the center of the wheel, then use it to help make uniform roundovers on the edges. Use the gouge just as you would to turn a bead.

the top left photo on p. 48. Drill a hole the width of your wheel in scrapwood or medium-density fiberboard (MDF), then cut it in half.

4 Add details. Swing the rest around to support the tools better. It's easiest to add simple detailing with a skew chisel. Grooves are easiest to turn with the skew chisel long point, keeping the tool flat on the rest, as shown below.

Adding details also gives you an opportunity to recycle old tools to create unique cutters. For example, the photo at right shows a tool I made from a nearly worn-out scraper on the corner of a high-speed grinding wheel.

TIRE GAUGE. A simple template like the one shown here makes it easy to create uniform round-overs on the wheels.

RECYCLED. I reground a worn scraper to give it more life as a grooving tool. Unique cutters make your turnings distinctive.

CUT IN DETAILS. Pivot the tool rest and use a skew to add grooves and other details.

FINISHED. This pair of finished wheels are also seen on page 56. I've hidden the dark burnish mark against the wheely-bug body.

How to Turn Cross-Grained Wheels

Wheels that are thin or more than 3 in. (75mm) in diameter will be stronger if the grain runs at 90 degrees to the lathe axis. Plywood is also a good option for strength. However, having the grain running across the face means the wood is harder to cut cleanly. As with all small-diameter facework, the main problem is coping with the endgrain that comes around twice each revolution.

The photos in this section show a cross-grained wheel that I turned from a decades-old piece of builder's waste. The board had not warped, so I bored a hole at the center of the blank and wound it onto a screw chuck. I use plywood spacers to shorten the effective length of the chuck's screw to about ⅜ in. (9mm), which is all you need most of the time. The wider the faceplate is in relation to the blank, the shorter the screw can be.

If you cut cross-grained wheel blanks from dimensioned boards with parallel faces and drill the axle hole square to the faces, then you can easily turn the wheels between cones. Simply bring them down to size and round the edges. However, if you want to add details to the wheels, you have better access to the face if you use a screw chuck.

1. With the blank screwed tightly against the chuck, true up the face (see the top photo at right). Check that it's slightly concave, so it will sit firmly against the chuck when you reverse it (see the bottom photo at right). A skewed scraper is the best tool to use if the face is already reasonably flat. Note that the edge is slightly radiused so you cannot have both corners contacting the wood at once. Otherwise, a bowl or spindle gouge is a better option to true the face before finishing with the scraper. (*Never* use a big deep-fluted spindle-roughing gouge: They are not designed for facework.)

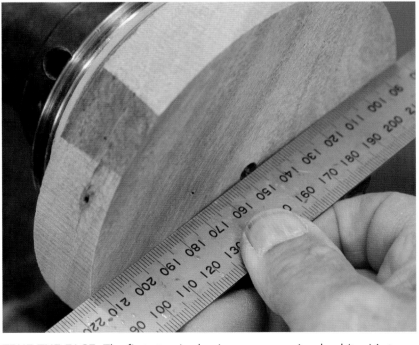

TRUE THE FACE. The first step in shaping a cross-grain wheel (top) is to make the face slightly concave, so that it will fit snugly against the chuck when you reverse it. Use a ruler to check the profile (above).

MARK THE DIAMETER. Set the dividers to the diameter you want, then use the left point to score the wood. When the score mark lines up with the right point, you've got the diameter. Don't let the right point touch the wood.

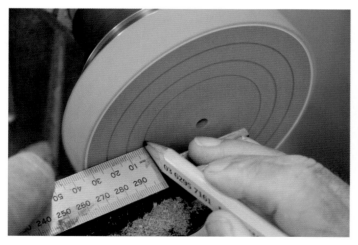

LAY OUT DETAILS. Set out the detail, measuring from the diameter you just marked. You can turn the detail using either a skew chisel like a scraper or a square-end scraper.

SAND AND FINISH. With the face completed, sand it smooth and apply a finish.

SCREW CHUCK. Reverse the wheel, so that the finished side faces the screw chuck.

2 Use dividers to lay out the diameter of the wheel, as shown in the top photo on the facing page. The circle you score with the left point needs to line up with the right point, but don't let the right point touch the wood.

3 Lay out, turn, and finish this face. I marked lines for the details by measuring from the diameter marked with the dividers (see the bottom left photo on the facing page). To turn the detail, I used a skew chisel flat on the rest like a scraper. It was more effective than the skewed scraper used to true the face. With the details cut, sand and finish this face (see the bottom right photo on the facing page).

4 Reverse the blank on the screw chuck (see the photo at left). Lay out the width of the wheel, working from the face against the chuck. But before you bring the wheel down to size, true the face back to the desired thickness using a scraper (see the photo below).

TRUE THE SECOND FACE. Use a skewed scraper and take light cuts to raise more dust than shavings. This face will be the inside of the wheel, so it is best made slightly convex.

TURN TO SIZE. Mark the diameter with dividers, then turn the wheel to size. Here, I'm using a ⅜-in. (9mm) detail gouge.

5 Lay out the diameter on the face, then establish the diameter, working to the lines on each face. Use a gouge to cut in from either face (see the photo at left). After you've finished with the gouge, refine the surface by shear-scraping with the scraper held at an angle (see the photo below left). It helps if the scraper has a honed edge. To avoid a catch, it's essential to keep the cut in the bottom half of the scraper.

6 Round over the rims by using a spindle gouge as a shear scraper, as shown in the photo below. The gouge must be held on its side with the flute facing the wood you are cutting. Stroke the surface with small arcing cuts, which you make by dropping the tool handle slightly. Mirror the cut for the other corner. Sand and finish everything you didn't do earlier.

SMOOTH THE RIM. If necessary, use a scraper to refine the surface. To avoid a catch when shear scraping with the tool tilted up, keep the cut in the bottom half of the scraper, where you see the dust.

ROUND OVER THE EDGES. Use a spindle gouge on its side as a shear scraper to make a series of small arcing cuts to round over the edges of the wheel.

FIXING TEAROUT. If you get tearout around an axle hole (left), remove it by first marking the area to be turned out. Then use a square-end scraper to bore in far enough to leave a clean surface (below). You'll need to include this detail on every wheel in the set.

A Final Note

When I unscrewed the cross-grain wheel, I spotted some tearout around the hole on the first side (see the top photo). This often happens with hardwoods or when the hole for the screw could have been a bit wider. I circled the damaged area and turned away the tearout using a ¾-in. square-end scraper (see the photo above). Any other wheels in the set will have to match this new feature, of course.

PROJECTS

WHEELY BUG   56

RACING CAR   65

PEGGIES   72

WANDS   80

STACKERS   88

SPHERES   98

FRUIT & VEGETABLES TO "CUT"   106

CROQUET SET   115

TEETHER & RATTLE   122

NESTING TUBS   131

GOBLET   139

BILBOQUET   146

SPINNING TOPS   152

BALANCE TRAY   159

TABLE SKITTLES   166

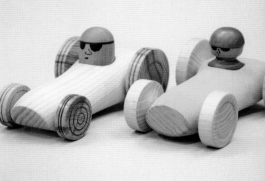

WHEELY BUG

The previous chapter showed you how to make wheels, so in this chapter and the next we'll make a couple of toys that need wheels. First is a bug-like critter for toddlers to take for a walk, dragging it along by a cord. Its ancestors are creatures somewhere between fish and dinosaurs, and its wheels are turned between centers. The second,

in the next chapter, is a racing car complete with driver; its wheels are turned using a chuck. Each project offers the possibility of infinite variations if you unleash your own sense of whimsy, especially when it comes to decorating the final forms.

The Wheely Bug is simply a string of beads of varying sizes. There's a big elongated bead for

CONTRASTS. It's often good to use contrasting woods so different parts of a toy stand out. I turned these from reddish sheoak (endemic to Australia) and yellow-ish mulberry.

the body and a string of smaller ones for the tail. You can make the bug as long as you like. The pull cord passes through the body as well as the beads for the tail. To make the tail flexible, chamfer the ends of each connecting component (see the bottom right photo on p. 59). For stability, the width of the toy across the wheels needs to be about three times the diameter of the wheels.

Turn the Body

The blank for the body is slightly more than 2 in. (50mm) square and about 4 in. (100mm) long. The holes in the body—one for the axle, the other for the cord—need to be drilled accurately at right angles to each other. They must not intersect. The hole for the cord is used to hold the blank between two conical centers.

When preparing the blank for drilling, be sure that at least two sides are parallel and that the ends are at 90 degrees to those sides. If you drill into a tapered blank, the body will be askew on the axle. It's best to use brad-point drills that won't wander off-line, as standard twist drills often do.

1 Stand the blank on end and mark the center. To ensure accuracy, I use a center punch to make a starter hole for the drill.

2 Drill a ³⁄₁₆-in. (5mm) hole through the center for the cord. The hole needs to be spot-on at center all the way through the blank. If the drill wanders off, you will have to re-cut the sides to make them parallel to the center hole before drilling the hole for the axle. To do that, draw a line at each end from the side of the center hole at right angles to the top face, and connect the two. This creates a line parallel to the hole. Then draw another line parallel to it near the edge and cut along it (see the photo at right). Repeat the cut for the second face. Note that I keep my fingers clear of the saw blade by using a square block to support the blank as I cut the

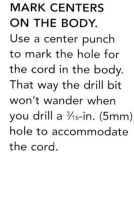

MARK CENTERS ON THE BODY. Use a center punch to mark the hole for the cord in the body. That way the drill bit won't wander when you drill a ³⁄₁₆-in. (5mm) hole to accommodate the cord.

SQUARE UP. If the hole for the cord ends up off-axis, trim two sides of the blank so that they are parallel with the hole.

DRILL AGAIN. When you make the hole for the axle, be sure it does not intersect the hole for the cord.

SHAPE THE BODY. You can use a skew chisel (top) or a spindle gouge (above) to form the elongated bead for the body of the bug.

wedge from the side. As an alternative, use a disk sander to bring the faces down to the lines parallel to the hole. Now the blank is ready for the axle hole.

3 On one of the parallel faces, draw a line parallel to the side of the center hole. Then lay the blank on the other of the two parallel sides and drill a hole for the axle. A ⅜-in. hole for an ¹¹⁄₃₂-in. axle (a 9.5mm hole for a 9mm axle) should work well. Drill the hole next to the line and away from center. I make the axle hole slightly toward the head of the bug, but the location isn't critical.

4 Mount the body section between a conical drive and a conical revolving tail center and turn the body. Use either a skew chisel or spindle gouge. Sand the body at this stage, but don't apply any finish until you've put on the face and any other artwork.

Turn the Tail

The beads that comprise the tail are best made from a spindle blank cut into short, bead-sized, squared lengths. This allows you to keep the grain pattern running through the tail.

BODY PARTS. When you cut blanks for the beads that make the bug's tail, keep them in order so that the grain pattern will run smoothly from end to end.

DRILL BEAD BLANKS. Drill into the endgrain for the hole for the cord and chucking. You don't need to have the holes dead-center.

SIZING THE TAIL. To be sure the tail beads taper smoothly down to the end, measure the diameter of one bead and use that to size the next bead on the string.

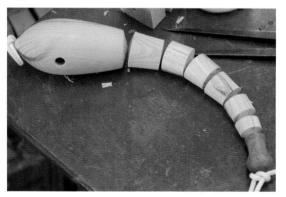

TAKING SHAPE. String the tail beads to check their size and shape. If one looks too large, put it back on the lathe and trim it. Note how the ends of the beads are chamfered so the tail can waggle.

1 Drill each blank on a drill press so that you have a vertical hole pretty much at center. These holes don't have to be spot-on. I do this by eye. The more you measure by eye, the better you get at it. In a situation like this, it's easy to accommodate the odd inaccuracy.

2 Mount a blank between conical centers. You can turn away the corners in seconds using a gouge, but it's even faster to take a peeling cut with a skew chisel flat on the tool rest. Just raise the handle to pivot the edge into the wood. When you get it right, each cut lasts only about three seconds. If you push the edge in straight, it will snag a shoulder and stop the blank from spinning. Peeling cuts are exhilarating and a great way to develop a lightness of touch.

As you turn each segment of the tail, gauge its diameter in relation to the previous segment.

Begin by measuring the tail end of the body and turn a cylinder to that diameter before shaping it. Finish the bead by chamfering the ends. When you've turned a segment, store it on a cord so you can watch the tail take shape.

If you find a bead a bit too large or not quite the right shape, it's easy enough to pop it back between centers and rework it. You don't even need to switch off the lathe as you take each segment on and off. Don't be afraid of catches. The wood stops if the tool grabs it, so there's only ever minimal damage. If you need to remove only small amounts or round a shoulder, 120-grit sandpaper usually does the job very nicely.

Designwise, the last bead looks better if it's either a different wood, a different shape, larger than the others, or all of those things. In time, the contrasting woods will mellow to be much the same tone.

TURN THE WHEELS. Once you've turned the cylinder, flatten a face. Then use dividers to mark the width from that face.

Turn the Wheels

The wheels can be about the same diameter as the body or even slightly larger. Here, I've made the wheels from a square with a 9mm hole for the axle that will go through the 9.5mm hole drilled in the body. Or try a $^{23}\!/_{64}$-in. axle for a $^{3}\!/_{8}$-in. hole.

1 Begin by reducing the drilled square blank to a cylinder, and measure the diameter with calipers. Then flatten one face with either a ½-in. (13mm) spindle gouge or a skew-chisel long point.

2 Lay out the width of the wheel, flatten its other face, and shape the wheel.

SHAPE THE RIM. A shopmade radius gauge helps you turn matching wheels.

ADD FINISH. After sanding, apply your finish of choice. I prefer to wipe on boiled linseed oil.

3 Sand and finish the wheel.

4 Turn the matching wheel in exactly the same way, using the same tools in the same order and with the same technique. Otherwise, you'll find it very difficult to match the second wheel with the first. Save any improved techniques for the next pair.

Turn the Axle, Fit the Wheels

The eventual width of this toy (the body plus the wheels) is about 4 in. (100mm), so I begin with a blank 5 in. (125mm) long. Axles less than 6 in. (150mm) long are easiest to turn when held in a chuck fitted with pin jaws.

1 Begin with half the blank protruding from the chuck. Turn away the exposed corners, tapering the end so the wheel just fits over it. Your aim is to ease the wheel over the end of the axle firmly enough to leave a burnish mark. This is the exact diameter that fits into the wheel.

2 Turn the spindle to the diameter of the burnish mark and fit the wheel. If you see two burnish marks (which often happens because you have the wheel slightly crooked), the diameter you need is halfway between the two.

3 With the wheel on the axle, mark the position of the inside so you know where to stop applying adhesive. Reverse the axle in the chuck so that the line you've just made is slightly proud of the jaws. Fit the second wheel, using the same steps and techniques you did for the first.

4 When it comes to assembling the wheels and body, I fix one wheel on the axle and let the adhesive set before putting the axle through the body and fixing the other wheel. When the glue has set, cut away the excess axle and finish the hub. Typically I'll start sanding with 80-grit

SIZE THE AXLE. Ease the wheel over the tapered end of the axle firmly enough to leave a burnish mark. That indicates the exact size you need to fit into the wheel.

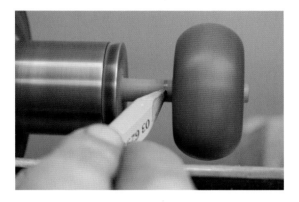

MARK THE AXLE. Mark where the inside of the wheel fits, so you can apply adhesive only where needed.

CLEAN UP THE WHEELS. Trim away the excess axle (left), then sand the face smooth (bottom) and touch up the finish.

and finish with 240-grit, then apply some boiled linseed oil as a finish.

String the Segments and Add the Eyes

Use a fairly stiff cord to string the segments together, otherwise you'll have a real problem poking it through the body. The white braided polyester lacing cord seen holding the beads in the background of the photo below is ideal but rather dreary; it's ³⁄₁₆ in. (4mm) in diameter. The shoelace shown in the foreground looks more interesting, but as you can see I had to use a small crochet hook to pull it through the hole.

You need a good knot to keep the beads on the cord. I favor the figure-eight shown in the top left photo on the facing page. Begin threading at the end of the tail, and put a knot where the cord emerges from the mouth. The tail looks best if it's a bit floppy, so don't pull the cord too tight. Put a large bead at the end of the cord to serve as a knob; keep it in place with a knot on either side.

With the parts assembled but the wheels not yet glued in place, I lay out the eyes, drill them, and draw the rest of the face. Now you can apply finish.

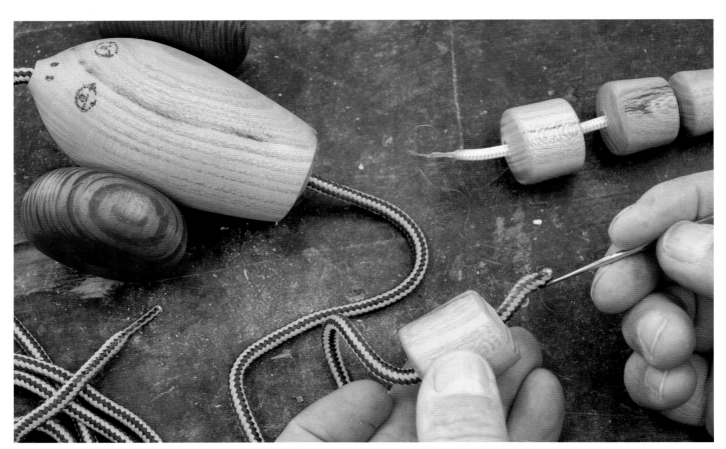

STRING THE BEADS. Thin synthetic cord (top right) works but offers little visual interest. A shoelace looks better but may be harder to thread through the holes.

QUICK KNOT. A figure-eight knot will keep the beads on the cord.

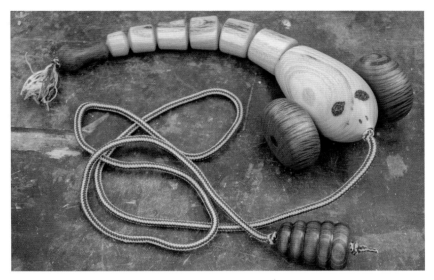

MORE KNOTS. Tie the cord where it emerges from the mouth and again to hold a bead at the end. Deliberately fraying the cord is a nice touch at the end of the tail.

HERE'S LOOKING AT YOU. Try making the eyes with a brad-point drill or small Forstner bit (left). Color in the small center hole with a marker (above). These eyes obliterated the originals in the photo top right.

A PAIR OF SNAILS

This easy project yields a couple of snails to roll along in the company of your Wheely Bug. From one blank you get a pair of off-center turnings, but without turning off-center or the associated vibration. The snails are essentially a couple of large beads that are easily turned using a skew chisel or long-beveled detail gouge.

You need a short board about 5 in. (130mm) square and 1½ in. (40mm) thick. Draw a centerline with the grain along one face and mark and punch the center on each end. Then sketch a snail on the upper half; outline the profile with a marker so the outline will be clearly visible when the wood is spinning. You can drill the axle holes before or after the blank is turned.

When you've finished the turning and sanding, cut down the center of the blank, and shape the bottom. Curving the underside makes a snail more snail-like at rest and prevents its tail from dragging when it's pulled along.

For the wheels (see Chapter 6), turn flattened hemispheres to match the snail's body. Do all the painting and decorating before you glue the wheels in place.

Finally, add a large bead to the end of the cord to serve as a handle, holding it with two knots. The hidden end of the pull cord is knotted and tucked into a hole drilled into the base at right angles to the mouth hole.

THESE SNAILS ROCK AND ROLL. Making these snails is a simple exercise in turning.

LAY OUT THE BLANK. Outline one snail's body with a marker and mount the blank between centers. You can drill the axle holes before or after you've done the turning.

TURN TO THE LINE. The heavy outline should be clearly visible when you power up the lathe. Use a gouge or a skew chisel to turn to the line.

RACING CAR

This is a project turned off-center that needs to be mounted accurately on the lathe. Because the blank is mounted well off-center, the tool isn't in contact with the wood when the gap comes around. You need to move the cutting edge of the tool on a smooth trajectory regardless of whether there is wood or space against the bevel.

It's very good for your technique and, being small-scale, not nearly as dangerous or scary as it might seem.

If you've never done any off-center turning, I recommend getting some wood you don't mind wasting and have a few trial runs. Always wear a face shield to protect yourself in case the blank flies off the lathe.

VROOM! The racer on the left has a body made from mulberry and forest sheoak wheels. The two-seater has a sheoak body and osage orange wheels.

TEST TRACK. Practice off-center turning on pieces of scrap before you start turning the real thing.

MARK THE BLANK. Draw a centerline down one face and the end, and then mark the center and front edge of the hole for the driver.

The blank needs to be about 6 in. long, 2¼ in. wide, and 2 in. thick (150mm by 60mm by 50mm). The blank used here is some sort of softwood cut from an old pallet. To ensure accurate layout and drilling, be sure that opposing sides are parallel and the ends are square to the sides.

Turn the Body

1 Draw a line down the center of the top face and on each end. A center-finding ruler is a great help. Then draw a line across the blank to mark the front of the driver's hole. Its exact location isn't critical, but the toy looks best if the driver is close to the rear. The mark crossing the centerline in front of the ruler indicates the center of the hole, which I've placed 2 in. (50mm) from the rear.

2 Carry the line for the front of the driver's hole over to one side of the blank. Mark a line at about a 10-degree angle from that spot to the rear of the blank, then shade in an area representing the driver's hole at right angles to the angled line. Cut away the wedge and redraw the centerline on the new surface.

3 Lay out the axle positions, leaving at least ⁷⁄₁₆ in. (10mm) of wood in the base. The centers of my 9.5mm holes are ⅝ in. (15mm) from the bottom and 1 in. (25mm) in from each end. You can see the marks for the centers in the top photo on the facing page. When laying out the axle holes, be sure that the rear axle hole does not intersect with the driver's hole.

4 Drill the driver's hole. To make that part of the blank horizontal, either slide the wedge offcut under the blank on the edge of the drill table, or hold the blank in a vise. Be sure to set the depth stop on the drill press so you don't bore through the base.

SLICE A WEDGE.
Mark an angled line
at the top and shade
where the driver's
hole will go. Cut away
the wedge. The blank
is also marked to
show the centers of
the axle holes.

**DRILL FOR THE
DRIVER.** Support the
blank either with the
offcut wedge (shown)
or in a vise to orient it
properly when drilling
the driver's hole.

DRILL AGAIN. Flip the blank and drill the holes for the axles.

BODY SHAPE. To get a sense of the shape the car body will take, turn the blank slowly by hand while you hold a pencil on the endgrain.

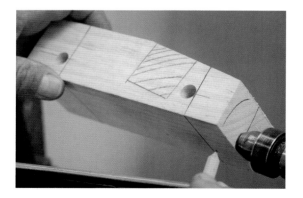

5 Drill holes for the axles, making sure they are parallel to the base of the car (photo above).

6 Mount the blank. Be sure to get the centers exactly on the lines you drew in step 1. Moving the centers toward the top or bottom of the blank determines the shape the car body will take when you turn it. Because the front end will be nearly round, I locate the drive level with the front axle so the wheels will be on the maximum body width. At the other end I locate the tail center as near the bottom as I can, using a cup center to prevent the grain from splitting. You can get an idea of the shape by holding a pencil to the endgrain as you rotate the blank by hand. The curve on the endgrain is very tight, which looks okay, but you need the full width of the blank for the rear axle, even retaining a hint of the flat side.

It helps to locate the axle holes by drawing lines adjacent to them. When the wood is spinning, lines are much easier to see than the holes.

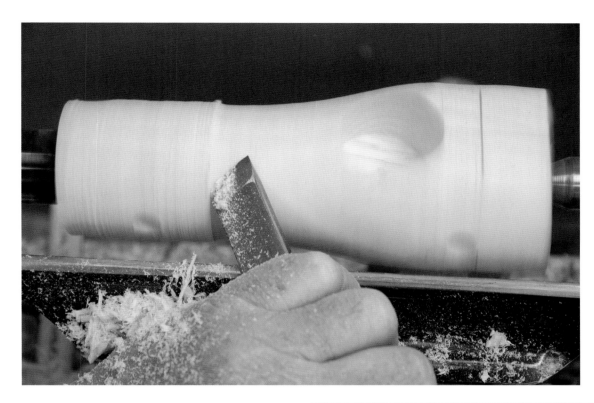

BODY WORK. Use either a spindle gouge or a skew chisel (shown) to shape the body.

7 Turn the body, starting at each end and working back toward the driver's hole with a series of scooping cuts. I do the rear first, turning the square edges back to the driver's hole. You can use a spindle gouge, a spindle-roughing gouge, or a skew chisel.

8 Sand the body, using a soft backing pad for the abrasive. The photo at right shows me using a thick block of neoprene, but folded cloth also works well. *Never* wrap the abrasive or cloth around your hand or fingers. Heavy sanding will soften all the corners, so, as with the turning and grinding, try to let the wood come to the abrasive. That means holding the abrasive steady so it doesn't bump into the gap too much as the flat base comes around. On flat sections, abrasives remove more from leading edges than trailing edges, so it helps to reverse-sand so each corner gets the same treatment—assuming your lathe can run in reverse.

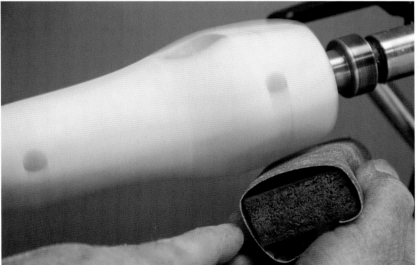

SMOOTH. Sand the body with the abrasive backed with a folded cloth or resilient pad.

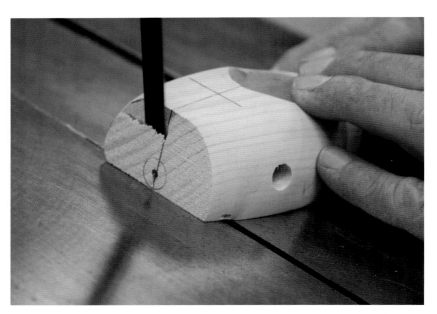

TRIM THE ENDS. Tilt the bandsaw table so you can trim the ends of the car body at an angle, removing the waste as you improve the shape.

FINAL SHAPING. Use a belt sander (shown) and a disk sander to bring the body to its final shape.

9 Finish shaping the body. Cut away each end to remove the chucking marks. If you tilt the bandsaw table to cut wedges off either end, you will maintain the overall length of the vehicle while removing defects and adding some style (see the photo at left). Complete the sloping front and rear ends on the belt sander, and clean up the flat area surrounding the rear axle on a disk sander.

Add the Wheels and Driver

Turn two sets of wheels (see Chapter 6). I think the toy looks more like a racing car if the rear wheels are larger and thicker than the front ones. It also looks better if the wheels are turned from wood that contrasts with the body.

With the wheels finished, turn axles as you would for the Wheely Bug in the previous chapter. Do a dry fit and test the wheels on a flat surface like a saw table. If one wheel fails to touch the table, reduce the size of its mate by putting it back on the lathe and peeling it down to size. See the next chapter for instructions on turning a driver for the car.

AN OPEN-AIR OMNIBUS

The bus is made essentially the same way as the racing car, following the same steps and using the same techniques. Of course, it needs to be longer; I used a piece of 2×4 (40mm×90mm) that was about 8½ in. (215mm) long.

Drill the passenger holes vertically into the wider face of the blank, spacing them so that they don't intersect with the axle holes. There's no need to saw away a wedge, as on the racing car.

On the lathe, shift the blank between centers three times, shifting one end at a time. That way, the body will have asymmetric curves; otherwise, you'll simply be rounding the sides of a flat board. Have fun exploring new shapes using inexpensive material. You're bound to have a few mishaps where you take away too much, but the journey is enjoyable, especially when you discover a new shape.

It may take some heavy sanding to soften the corners. Add color, a driver, and passengers, and you're en route.

MASS TRANSIT. Once you've mastered the racing car, you can try your hand at the bus. This one is made from pine.

PEGGIES

eggies, as you can see, are little people—some male and some female. Just as in real life, their profiles can vary dramatically, giving you plenty of leeway design-wise. This is your chance to create caricatures of people you know.

When small kids play, they mostly imitate real life as they use dolls, blocks, and action figures to act out journeys, visits, and conversations. A child's ability to transform even the most rudimentary or stylized figures into characters means that you need not be too worried

PLENTY OF PERSONALITY. Even though peggies are simple turnings, they can be decorated in infinite ways to make each one unique.

CLOSE RELATIVES.
The nine pins in a
skittles set are simply
large, identical
peggies.

about realism. Peggies need be little more
than cylinders with rounded tops or a knob
for a head.

When you turn figures, it's a good idea to
work to standard diameters so a figure that
arrives in one vehicle can leave in another.
Working to set diameters and heights also gives
you plenty of measuring practice. Hold the
blanks in a chuck so you can finish the head on
the lathe and save some sanding off the lathe.
Reckon on turning two figures about 2½ in.
(65mm) tall from a blank projecting 6 in.
(150mm) from the chuck. You can drill the stub
left in the chuck and later use it to make a bead
or small wheel.

The turning technique described here can
yield more than small figures. Skittles, for
example, are little more than elongated and
unadorned peggies.

Size and Wood

Toddlers will chew on anything, so if you're
making peggies for kids not yet three, what you
turn must be too big to swallow (see p. 5);
nothing too small and round. Keep those for
older kids. The figures fitting into the vehicles
on p. 65 are sized to fit easily into 1⅛-in.
(30mm) and 1⅜-in. (35mm) holes.

Unless you are prepared to paint the whole
peggie, look for bland wood with barely discern-
able annular rings, a pale wood that offers a
clean surface for the artwork. In suburbia, you
might find suitable fruitwoods or small orna-
mental trees and shrubs like lilac, rhododen-
dron, and cotoneaster. Commercially, look
for pale mahoganies, maple, cherry, poplar,
and pine.

TRUING THE END.
Start by pivoting the skew chisel long point into the wood, then raise the handle to cut with the edge as you near the center, slowing the cutting rate all the way.

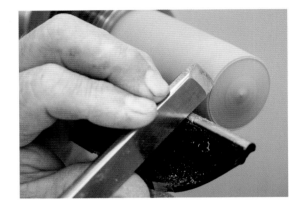

MULTIPURPOSE GAUGE. A simple shopmade gauge makes it easy to size the peggies. Drill two identical holes in a piece of scrap and saw across one so you have a half-circle to gauge diameter as you're turning (shown) and a hole to check that the cylinder fits in another component.

Turning a Peggie

1 True the blank, and don't forget the end. Truing endgrain is always a good opportunity to practice cuts you might try to avoid, especially with a skew chisel. Start by raising the handle to pivot the long point into the wood.

Cut almost to the center using the long point, with only the bevel side in contact with the wood. Then as you come to center, raise the handle slightly to start cutting with the edge, keeping the cut just behind the point of the tool, as shown at left. With most woods, you should get a small hat-like conical shaving. To avoid tearout near the center, slow the pace of the cut until you stop at the center. If you try to use the skew point the whole way, chances are you'll end up with a small tenon, and if you push at that, you'll pull out the endgrain and need to start over.

2 Size and check the diameter of the cylinder. I use homemade gauges in conjunction with a skew chisel. The skew is kept flat on the rest for a peeling cut as the gauge drops over the cylinder. If you want your peggies to fit into passenger holes in vehicles, it's a good idea to stop the lathe and check the diameter with a test hole.

3 Turning the head is a great opportunity to practice bead cutting using a skew chisel. Start the skew long-point-up and use the short corner to make the cut. As you roll the skew, you also move it along the rest to keep the tool almost square to the lathe axis. Halfway to center, chances are you'll lose sight of the short corner and therefore the cut; pull the tool away from the wood, turn it over, and use the long point to complete the cut.

BEAD WITH A SKEW. To make a bead with a skew chisel, begin with the long point up, so the short corner does the cutting. Continue until you're about halfway through the cut (top). Then flip the tool so the long point is down (above left) and complete the cut (above right).

If you use a ½-in. (13mm) spindle gouge instead of a skew, roll the tool in the direction of the cut so that it ends up on its side with the bevel rubbing all the way.

A bead head is most easily turned using a gouge rather than a skew chisel. That's because the neck involves turning a cove. As you cut in from either side to create a neck, keep an eye on the emerging head, moving the cove down the body if the head looks a bit flat. Or you can

BEAD WITH A GOUGE. Begin the cut with the tool's flute at about the one o'clock position (left). Roll the tool as you move through the cut. The gouge should be nearly on its side when you finish.

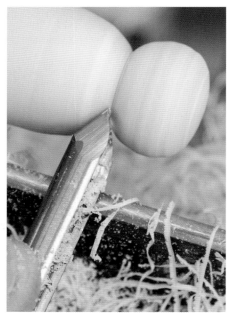

BEGINNING A BEAD HEAD. Use a gouge to shape a cove, working from the right and then the left.

FINISHING A BEAD HEAD. Once you've established the cove for the neck, round over both sides to change the shape, creating a bead for the head and shoulders for the body. To avoid a catch, be sure the gouge is on its side at the end of each cut.

reduce the diameter. At the bottom of each cut the gouge needs to be right on its side to avoid a catch. If you roll the tool too far at the end of the cut, you can catch the top wing.

To suggest a hat brim, begin by using a ½-in. (13mm) skew chisel flat on the rest for a peeling cut to shape the crown (photo below). Clean up the top of the brim by rotating the bevel side gently into the endgrain. Create the underside of the brim by pivoting the skew long point into the wood, then taking a shear cut with the short corner. You can also get under the brim with a peeling cut, or you can use a spindle gouge for a shear cut.

STARTING A HAT. Peeling cuts with a skew chisel will shape the crown and define the top of the hat brim.

FINISHING THE HAT. Use a skew long point to mark the bottom of the brim, then take shear cuts with the short corner (top). Or, with a gouge, take shear cuts, keeping the bevel rubbing on the wood (above).

SHAPING THE BODY. Refine the shape below the neck. A short tenon on the bottom of a peggie will make it female or someone wearing a coat.

PART OFF. Use a parting tool to undercut the base and separate the peggie. Remove the nubbin at the center with a chisel or sandpaper.

4 Complete the body, using a skew chisel for the best finish by far. At left, a peeling cut with a skew narrows the base to hint at legs emerging from a dress or coat, making this peggie female or someone wearing a coat.

5 Sand, then part off the peggie using a parting tool. Now you're ready to give the peggie a personality.

The Artwork

Don't let decorating the wood make you nervous. It's no big deal if you mess up because it's easy to sand back to clean wood and start again. Keep in mind that you're not looking for realism. Faces on peggies can be as simple as a computer smiley—☺—a couple of dots for eyes, plus a couple of lines for the nose and mouth. For the peggie in the photo shown on the facing page, the sunglasses are simply a couple of Ds hanging off a horizontal line, with a squiggle of a nose over a gash of a mouth—a sort of Joe Cool to sit in a sports car.

When decorating, it helps to rest your hands on something steady like the lathe bed or the bandsaw table.

If you want to draw or paint precise lines around your peggies, hold them in a chuck. I wrap rubber bands around the jaws to protect the wood, because you have to clamp it tight enough that your decorating hand doesn't dislodge it. Keep the lathe switched off and rotate the chuck by hand.

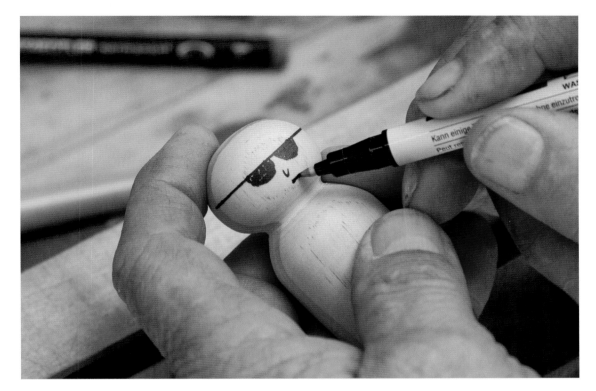

MAKE A FACE. Don't worry about drawing a face. A few simple lines is all it takes.

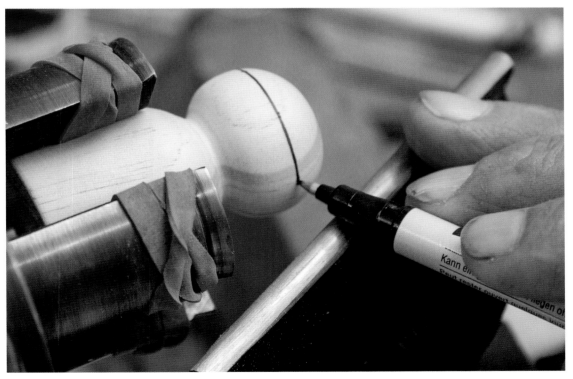

PRECISION. Hold a peggie in a chuck with rubber bands padding the jaws. For accurate lines around the cylinder, use the tool rest to steady a marker as you rotate the chuck by hand. Here, I'm drawing a line to represent the frame of sunglasses.

WANDS

All those young witches and wizards pottering through your life need a wand or two with which to cast their magic spells. Or maybe you know a budding magician for whom a wand is an essential prop that can transform scarves into a white rabbit or birds into a cat (all illusion of course, in case you're worried that the occult may be involved).

For any wood turner, wands provide wonderful skew-chisel practice. You are turning stubby little pointers with fancy handles. Bad catches or heavy spiral chatter marks might be retained as features that impart extra magic to the stick.

MYSTICAL STICKS.
Wands offer limitless design opportunities, from fully round sticks (left) to ones that retain some flat surfaces from the original blank (right).

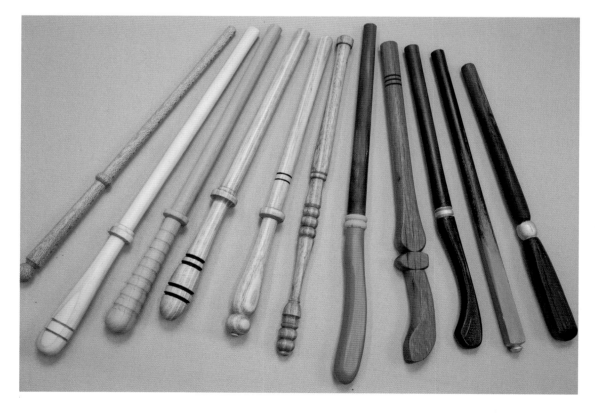

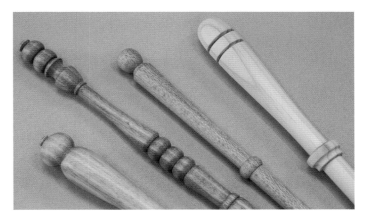

SIMPLE FORMS. These four handles are simply turned and polished with beeswax.

CHARRED AND BURNT. The top handle has been ebonized and rubbed back to look well used. The second down is charred to highlight the coves, and the others have charred grooves.

PAINTERLY. The top wand is a really rough bit of recycled wood that I wire-brushed before applying acrylic paint. The middle one is a simple turning with two paint colors blending together. At the bottom is an osage orange wand that I charred to highlight the end of the handle in relation to the turned bead.

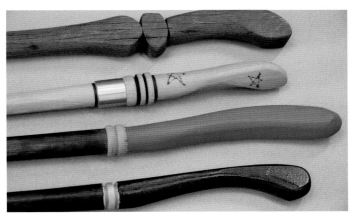

CARVED HANDLES. The blanks used for these wands were wedge-shaped, square at one end and rectangular at the other. This allows you to retain two flat sides to carve pistol-grip handles. You do the final shaping on the lathe with various sanders. The shiny band on the second wand down is a copper ferrule (which obviously adds enormous power to any wand).

Safety and Eyes

Remember that kids of all ages will be pointing and waving these wands. Don't make the ends so pointy that they'd poke out an eye or pierce the skin. Keep the pointy end at least ½ in. (15mm) in diameter, and hold the length to no more than 15 in. (380mm). Any longer and the wand becomes ever more dangerous when being waved around.

HAND SUPPORT.
Wrap the fingers of your free hand around the blank to prevent it from flexing. Here, my right hand pushes the tool against my thumb, which supports the blade as it moves along the rest.

You can turn anything from a smooth pointer emerging from a rough branch to a handle of massed beads and coves. You can embellish the wands by painting or charring, by adding beads, icons, and ferrules, or by inserting dots of contrasting material. Mostly it will be the handles that are decorated. The photos on the previous page show a few samples to set you on your way.

How to Turn a Wand

Use wood with straight grain that runs the length of the blank for strength. A wand blank needs to be ¾ in. to 1 in. (20mm to 25mm) in diameter. Mount the blank between a spur drive and revolving tail center. Be careful not to over-tighten the tailstock, which can bow the blank and lead to flexing and chatter marks. Use the tail center to *support* the work, not squeeze it.

1 Turn the square blank to a cylinder with either a spindle-roughing gouge or a skew chisel. Once you become confident with the skew, that's the tool you'll use because it delivers the best finish. For roughing and planing cuts, a 1-in. (25mm) or ¾-in. (20mm) skew is best; for beads, a ½-in. (12mm) skew might be easier to handle. You have to gain confidence to use a skew, of course, so do that by using one to turn an entire wand. (If you insist on using a gouge, see the photos on p. 32.)

To avoid chatter marks, use minimal tool pressure against the wood and use your free hand to support the blank, equalizing the pressure from the tool. You also need to keep your thumb in contact with the tool on the rest as a point of reference, as shown in the photo above. It may look dangerous, but in more than 35 years of teaching I've never seen anyone get cut using this technique. If there's a catch, the spindle will bounce or break and you start again. It's all part of the learning process. Your hand also serves as

ROUNDING THE BLANK. Use a skew chisel long-point-down when turning thin spindles, slicing with the edge.

REVERSE DIRECTION. To finish rounding the blank, flip the skew so the long point is up as you work toward the tailstock.

a built-in thermostatic pressure gauge. If it gets hot, that means you are pushing the tool too hard against the wood.

As always, begin turning the square section to round by taking a series of scooping cuts from one end to the other. It's most efficient to use the skew chisel long-point-down, so any pressure you put into the cut runs parallel to the lathe axis rather than against it. Chatter won't be a problem for the first couple of cuts, because

you're working near the drive. However, you will soon need to support the work with your hand.

Continue to make scooping cuts toward the headstock until you have nearly reached the end. Then flip the skew over and use it long-point-up to cut toward the tailstock and off the end (rather than come in from space). As the bottom photo above shows, the skew remains in my right hand and my thumb eases the tool along the rest and into the cut.

2 When the blank is round, define the length of wood you have to work with by peeling away the material surrounding the tail center. Leave about ¼ in. (6mm) of wood surrounding the tail-center cone, which prepares this end for parting off. Then round over the end.

3 Develop the handle. Use the skew-chisel long point to cut straight in and define the spot where the handle meets the shaft. Work up to that point, reducing the diameter of the wand, as shown in the photo below.

DEFINE THE HANDLE. Use the skew long point to cut a groove where the handle joins the rest of the wand. Then trim the handle to its final diameter, working up to the groove.

DEFINE THE END. Use the long point of a skew to trim the end at the tailstock (top). Then round the end, cutting with the skew's short corner (above).

ADD EMBELLISHMENTS. Turn your imagination loose to add details to the handle. Here, I begin with some grooves (top), followed by a couple of beads (above).

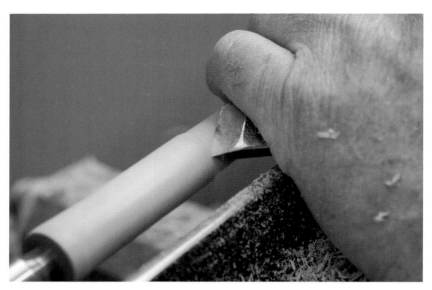

COMPLETE THE WAND. Use shearing cuts with a skew to bring the wand down to its final diameter and shape.

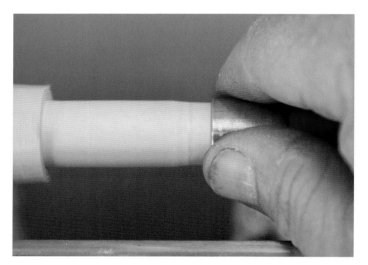

ADD SOME METAL. If you wish, fit a short length of copper tubing onto the wand for added pizzazz. Slide the tube onto the wood so it leaves a burnish mark, then turn the wand down to that diameter.

4 Add detail to the handle. I tend to go for less rather than more, so am content with a pair of grooves and a couple of beads to link the handle to the pointy end (see the photos on p. 85). I use the short corner of a ¾-in. (19mm) skew to turn the beads, but you might find a ½-in. (13mm) skew or detail gouge easier to manipulate.

5 Complete the wand using refined versions of your initial planing cuts when you roughed the blank to round.

If you fancy adding a metal ring, now is the time. Ease a short length of copper plumbing tubing onto the shallow taper of the wand's pointy end until it leaves a burnish mark. It's like fitting a ferrule to a handle or a lid to a suction-fit box. The burnish mark is the same diameter as the internal diameter of the tube. All you have to do is take light planing cuts down to that diameter, testing the fit frequently as you go. You don't need to stop the lathe, but remember that metal gets hot very quickly with friction. Use just enough pressure to make a mark, then back the tube off a tad while you do the turning. This finished wand is second down in the bottom right photo on p. 81.

Turning Soft Metal

You can trim the ends of copper or aluminum tubing on a wood lathe using a high-speed steel (HSS) scraper or skew chisel bevel side. Hold the pipe in pin jaws and run the lathe at about 1,200 rpm (see p. 173). Be sure to wear eye protection.

6 Sand and finish. Use abrasives to smooth away any small bumps in your turning. Maintain the cylindrical form by wrapping a length of abrasive along the wand; keep it moving to and fro along the length. While sanding I thought the handle looked a bit dull, so I decided to blacken the grooves using a wedge of dry hardwood. This finished wand is the third from the top in the top right photo on p. 81. To learn how to burn grooves in wood, see p. 178.

7 Part off the wand. Begin at the headstock end by turning a narrow groove and leaving just enough wood to keep the wand connected to the drive while you cut through at the tailstock end. Once the wand is off the lathe, saw off any waste and hand-sand the ends.

SAND SMOOTH. To smooth away any bumps, wrap a length of abrasive around the wand and keep it moving back and forth along the length up to the beads.

PART OFF. Begin at the headstock end, leaving just enough wood to keep the wand attached. Then cut it free at the tailstock end.

STACKERS

These things must have a name, so I've settled on stacker to describe this anthropomorphic variation on the classic stack of rings. A collection of rings with a head should keep toddlers occupied for hours as they develop hand–eye coordination and an appreciation of size. It's a sort of vertical jigsaw puzzle.

As you can see in the drawing on the facing page, a post fits into the base, and over that fits a tube and a set of rings ranging from 4 in. down to 2 in. (100mm to 50mm) in diameter. The head tops the stack. The project involves both facework and spindle turning. Every component is easy to re-chuck, so you can make adjustments when it's time to fit the parts together. Exact

TRIO. Three stackers, one not yet the sum of his parts. The ring and tube blanks are bored before they go on the lathe.

RING BLANKS.
Flatten at least one face of the ring blanks and ensure that the holes are perpendicular to that face. You may be able to fit multiple rings on one board.

dimensions are not too important because each component can be shortened or thinned as required to make everything fit satisfactorily. If left plain, the rings generally look better if they all come from the same piece of wood.

Prepare the Blanks

Cut the base and rings from thicknessed boards. For my stackers, I used some claret ash offcuts about 1 in. (25mm) thick. The base needs to be about 4 in. (100mm) in diameter and 1 in. (25mm) thick—enough to support the center post. In the largest blank, drill a center hole for a screw chuck. In each of the others, drill a 1¼-in. (30mm) hole right through the blank.

Use a drill press so the holes are perpendicular to at least one side. In the photo above, the white board with three holes was planed and thicknessed so that I could drill from either side. I cut the other blanks from a board with only one face flattened. I drew the circles to define the blanks on the rough face and drilled from that side. That way, the holes were at right angles to the sanded face.

For the center post, use a straight-grained piece around 8 in. long by ¾ in. square (200mm by 20mm). For the tube that will finish at about 1¼ in. (32mm) in diameter, use stock that is 1⅜ in. (35mm) square and as long as your bit can drill deep. For the head, use a piece 2 in. (50mm) square and 2⅜ in. (60mm) long.

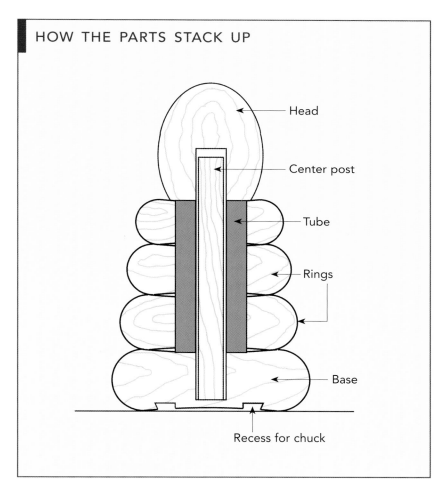

HOW THE PARTS STACK UP

- Head
- Center post
- Tube
- Rings
- Base
- Recess for chuck

TRUE FIRST. Begin shaping the base by truing the rim with a spindle gouge.

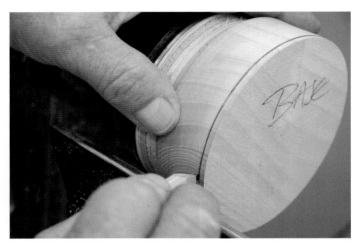

FLATTEN THE FACE. A pencil mark at the thinnest spot on the base will tell you how much to remove.

TWO CUTS. With a gouge on its side, cut back to the line near the rim. Then roll the gouge over and make a shear cut toward the center as shown.

Turn the Base

1 True the blank. This should become a habit, like fastening a seat belt in a car—something you do without thinking. First, true the profile with a spindle gouge, cutting in from either face to avoid tearing the endgrain.

Next, flatten the bottom of the blank. If you're not sure how much wood to remove, draw a pencil line at the thinnest point and cut back to that line. The most controlled method of removing this waste is to start the gouge on its side, then bring the edge into the cut by rotating the tool slightly clockwise as you drop the handle. Use your left hand to squeeze the edge toward the pencil line. When you've cut to the line, roll the gouge over for a shear cut, with the bevel rubbing, and head for the center.

2 Turn a recess for your chuck jaws. Before laying out the recess, smooth the base, making it slightly concave. My preferred tool on a near-flat face is a slightly radiused scraper. To avoid

SCRAPE IT SMOOTH. Use a scraper to smooth the face and make it slightly concave.

catches, tilt the tool down, so the angle between the top of the scraper and the surface you're cutting is less than 90 degrees, as seen below left.

If you don't have a special mini-scraper to turn a dovetailed recess, use a ½-in. skew chisel laid flat on the rest. Make sure the bottom of the recess is flat so the jaws have the best grip.

3 Sand the bottom of the base and apply your favorite finish. (If you plan to stain the wood, do only the sanding now.)

4 Remount the base on the expanding chuck jaws and turn the profile using a gouge. Turn the top very slightly concave so the stacking rings will sit flat on the base. And add some detail while you're at it to differentiate your work from store-bought.

SHAPING A RECESS. Use a skew chisel, as shown here, to make the recess for chuck jaws. Or you can use a small scraper designed for the job.

ADD UNIQUE DETAIL. Shaping the rim of the base is your chance to add fine touches that will set your work apart from the store-bought.

DRILL FOR THE POST. A Forstner or sawtooth bit will drill the cleanest hole. Wrap tape around the bit to show how deep to go.

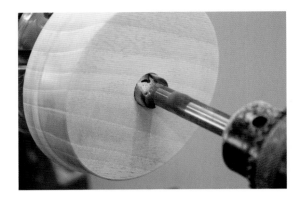

DRILL AGAIN. Use the same bit to drill out the center of the blank for the tube. Retract the bit frequently to clear out dust and shavings.

5 Drill a hole for the post, being careful not to go all the way through the base. The most accurate way to do this is to use a drill mounted in a Jacobs chuck in the tailstock with some tape as a guide as to how deep to drill. A Forstner or sawtooth bit is preferable because it leaves a flat-bottomed hole with smooth sides. A spade bit will also work but won't leave as clean a hole. Once you've drilled to the depth of the bit's head, retract the bit after four rotations of the handle so you can clear the dust that can clog the head. Use the same drill for this hole and the tube that goes over the center post.

6 Sand everything not already sanded and apply finish if you're leaving the wood unstained.

Make the Tube

1 Mount the blank for the tube in a chuck and turn the end to a cylinder. Bore the hole using the same bit you used for the post hole in the base (see the top photo at right).

2 With the hole drilled, reverse the blank in the chuck and turn the other end to round. (If it's too small for the chuck, just put it between centers.) If your drill wasn't long enough to go the all the way through, turn back to the hole. If the blank is too small for the chuck, cut it to length on a bandsaw. Remember, though, that it's dangerous to cut cylinders on a power saw unless the cylinder is mounted in a jig.

ROUND THE OTHER END. Use a skew chisel or spindle-roughing gouge to make the other end of the tube round.

GAUGE, PLANE, AND CHECK. Use a simple gauge or calipers to size the outside of the tube. Take a few light passes with a skew chisel to plane the surface smooth. Finally, use the gauge to check the tube's size, as shown.

3 Mount the drilled tube between cone centers (see p. 46 for more on this).

Turn the diameter a fraction smaller than the hole drilled in the rings. Use calipers or a gauge to size the cylinder. Begin with peeling cuts, then use a skew chisel to plane the surface. Before sanding, check that the tube will pass through the gauge or one of the ring blanks.

There's a good chance that you'll need to shorten the tube when it's time to assemble a stacker. In that case, pop the tube back between cones and turn away what is required to bring the tube level with the surrounding rings. On the other hand, if the tube is too short, replace it with two tubes half as long.

Make the Rings

The holes bored in the blanks enable you to hold them on small pin jaws if you have them, or you can make a jam chuck as shown at right. Jam-chucking is a very handy technique used for all manner of small jobs and when turning boxes with suction-fit lids. Once you get the hang of jam chucks you'll use them a lot.

1 To make the jam chuck, use a short length that has the grain running parallel to the lathe axis. A stub left in the chuck from some endgrain project is ideal. Turn the blank to a cylinder, then turn a tenon on one end to fit in a scroll chuck. Be sure to leave a small shoulder for the chuck jaws to sit against. On the opposite end, turn a tenon about ¾ in. (20mm) long for the jam chuck. Use a skew chisel flat on the rest for peeling cuts.

Size the tenon to match the hole in the ring blanks. Taper the tenon very slightly—about half a degree. Turn the lathe off and test the fit, holding the blank firm as you rotate the chuck by hand. The ring will leave a burnish mark, which defines the exact fit. Turn the inner portion of the tenon down to the burnish mark, but maintain a very shallow taper.

SIMPLE JAM CHUCK.
Turn a tenon on a piece of scrap to match the diameter of the holes drilled in the ring blanks.

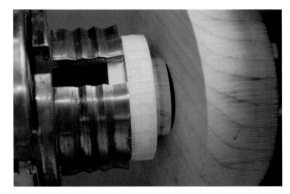

FINE-TUNING.
Rotate a ring blank over the tenon. That should leave a burnish mark (the dark ring), showing you the exact size the tenon needs to be.

JAM AND TRUE.
Fit the first ring on the jam chuck and true it with a gouge. This one was just a bit smaller than the base, so I removed only enough to make it a cylinder.

2 Jam the blank on the tenon, flat side first if it doesn't come from a thicknessed board. As you push the blank on, you'll feel it getting tighter. Be sure the blank seats against the tenon shoulder so that it will run true without any messing about on your part. True and shape the ring with a spindle gouge.

MARK THE WIDTH. Here, I'm using a ruler and modified dental tool in lieu of dividers to scribe the desired width of the ring.

FLATTEN THE RING. A scraper makes it easy to bring the ring down to size and make the face slightly concave.

ROUND THE RIMS. Mark guidelines on the rim and face, as shown here, then round over one side up to those lines. Repeat on the other face.

SCRIBE THE WIDTH. Vernier calipers make it easy to mark the rings for uniform graduations in size.

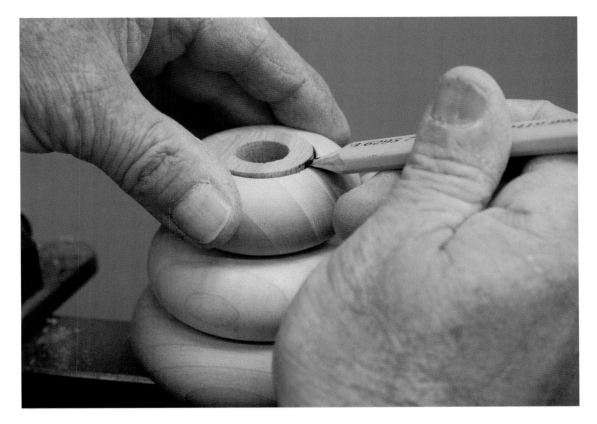

TRIM THE TUBE.
The tube should not project past the last ring. If necessary, pop it between cones and turn it down to size.

3 Mark the width of the ring. If you don't have dividers, use a ruler and pencil or even a converted dental tool as a scriber (as shown in the top left photo on the facing page). Use a slightly radiused scraper to remove the waste. Note that only a portion of the edge is used at one time. Make the face slightly concave.

4 Mark the center from the edge of the ring, and then lines ⅜ in. (10mm) in from the rim on each face. Round the corners using a gouge on its side, shear-cutting. This is facework, so to cut with the grain you work from smaller to larger diameter. And as these are shear cuts without the bevel rubbing, the edge is stroking the wood as the tool moves toward the center-line. Hold the tool almost on its side to avoid a heavy catch. When you have finished one side, mirror the cut on the opposite.

Make the other rings in exactly the same way, turning each new one slightly smaller than the last. I make each ring ½ in. (15mm) smaller in diameter than the one beneath; I find this easiest to calculate and mark using Vernier calipers (see the bottom right photo on the facing page). I measure each diameter, then close the caliper jaws an additional ½ in. (15mm). Because it's easy to pop a ring on and off the chuck, it's easy enough to mark the required diameter on each face; then you can size the diameter with those two lines as guides.

As you complete each ring, add it to the stack to see if the progression in size looks right. You can always put a ring back on the jam chuck to trim it a bit. When you have completed the final ring, shorten the tube if necessary.

CENTER POST. Establish the desired diameter in several places, then turn the post down to size.

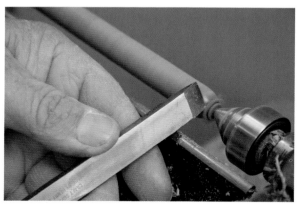

SMOOTH AND STYLE. Planing cuts with a skew chisel will smooth the post (center). Then you can round over or turn a bead on the end (above).

Turn the Center Post

The center post is a simple cylinder that fits snugly into the base and is long enough to project past the topmost tube, where it holds the stacker's head. Err on the side of caution regarding the length of the post. It's easy enough to shorten, so being too long is no big deal.

1 Round the blank, then use calipers to set the diameter (photo at left).

2 Smooth the cylinder using a skew chisel. Check that it will pass through the tube. If you like, decorate one end to define the top.

Turn the Head

1 Fix the blank in the chuck, turn the square to round, and true the endgrain. Then assemble the remaining parts and measure how far the center post protrudes (see the top left photo on the facing page). Drill the head blank to accept the post, using the same bit as you did for the base.

2 Turn the head, testing as you go to see how it looks against the body. (Be sure to switch off the lathe when you test). Sand and finish the head, then part it off.

Re-Chucking

If you don't like the head or its proportions, you can always make a jam chuck for re-turning. You can re-chuck and refine the shape of any piece of a stacker. For example, in the photo on p. 88, you can see that the claret ash stacker ended up with a rounded base. I changed it because when I held the body up to the head it was obvious the base didn't belong with the fat rings. It's always handy to be able to get work back on the lathe for adjustments.

HOLE IN THE HEAD. Measure how far the post extends past the tube. Use tape to mark that length on the bit, then drill a hole for the post in the head blank.

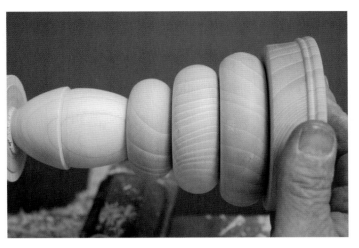

CHECK THE SHAPE. As you turn the head, check it with the rest of the stacker to see how the parts look all together. Here, the head seemed fine but the base didn't look right, so I rounded it to match the rings.

COLOR AND PART OFF. The blue and red concentric rings were easy to add before I parted off the head. Afterward, I sanded the end and touched up the color.

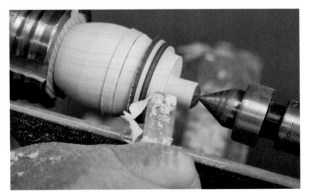

RE-CHUCKING. You can always re-chuck the head to refine its shape (center). Here, I decided to make the hat much shorter, and I'm using the tail center to hold the head onto the jam chuck (above). I can rework the face if there's a tiny shoulder on the hat for the chuck to grip.

SPHERES

S mall spheres, otherwise known as balls, are an essential part of several games in these projects. Getting a perfectly round ball, like a billiard ball, takes a lot of practice. You'll be relieved to know that perfect roundness isn't demanded here, especially where the balls aren't going to be rolled.

Turning a sphere requires accurate (if not perfect) measuring and turning with absolutely dry and well-seasoned wood if it is going to

SPHERES. As well as being central to many games, natural wood balls are decorative and interesting in themselves. They are very satisfying to turn.

SOLITAIRE SETS. Turned by Englishman Jason Breach, these solitaire sets are a great way to use up scraps of exotic wood. The balls on the natural-edge coolibah board (left) are 1¾ in. (45mm) in diameter; the board is 26 in. (660mm) wide. On the English olive ash board, the balls are 1½ in. (38mm) in diameter; the board is 20 in. (510mm) across.

remain spherical. In addition, you'll need a couple of jam chucks, which are easy to make yourself. A sphere involves both centerwork and facework—and occasionally something halfway between the two when the wood isn't always that easy to cut. A commercial sphere-cutting jig (see p. 104) can do a lot of the work with absolute accuracy, but it still leaves a nub that you must remove with the sphere jammed in a chuck.

The ball turned in this chapter is 2⅜ in. (60mm) diameter. You can start with the blank either in a chuck or between centers before transferring it to the jam chucks.

Turn a Sphere Freehand

1 Turn a cylinder with the same diameter as the ball you want to make. If the blank is in a chuck, flatten the end. You can get away with a slightly convex endgrain, but concavity will lead to a smaller ball than you may want.

Next, mark the cylinder's diameter as a length on the cylinder. Measure from the end if the blank is in a chuck. If it's mounted between

centers, make allowances for the centers penetrating the endgrain and position the ball accordingly. Define the length with a parting cut (or two cuts if you are working between centers).

MARK THE CYLINDER. Use a parting tool to define a cylinder that is equal in length to the cylinder's diameter.

ADD MORE GUIDE-LINES. Use a hard and sharp pencil to divide the cylinder into four equal portions. On the ends, divide the radius in half.

2 Mark the center and then subdivide the two halves. This divides the length of the cylinder into four equal parts. The finer the lines, the more accurately you can work, so a 4H pencil is better than a 3B. (The lines you see here are thick so they will show up better in the photo.)

On this 60mm diameter, I end up with lines $^{19}/_{32}$ in. (15mm) apart on the cylinder. On the endgrain, mark half the radius.

3 Turn flat facets between the lines at either side of center and the circles on the end-

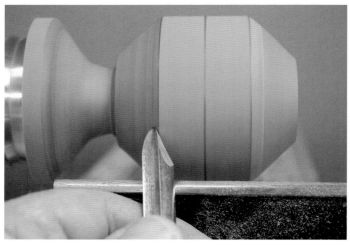

ANGLE THE ENDS. Turn facets between the lines at either side of center and the circles on the endgrain.

PREPARE TO PART OFF. When working between centers, part away most of the waste at either end of the ball-to-be. Then, off the lathe, saw away the waste.

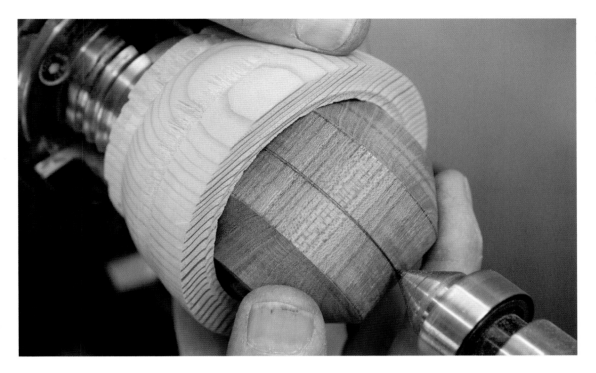

MAKE A JAM CHUCK. **Turn a chuck for the faceted blank. Align the original centerline with the tailcenter.**

grain. Part off the blank if it's held in a chuck. If it's mounted between centers, part nearly through at each end. Then, with the blank off the lathe, saw away the waste on each end.

4 Turn a jam chuck to hold the partially turned ball. You'll need a blank about one-third larger in diameter than the ball. The chuck needs to be slightly tapered inside, and marginally deeper than it is wide so the ball doesn't bottom out. Press-fit the part-turned ball into the chuck with the original centerline in line with the tail center (photo above).

5 Begin shaping the sphere by turning down to the original centerline. The aim is to retain the pencil line while removing the flats on either side. This is now facework, so the cleanest cuts are made by working from smaller to larger diameter. You can do most of this turning with shear-scraping cuts using a ⅜-in. (9mm) spindle or detail gouge. The bevel doesn't contact the wood as the edge strokes the surface.

BEGIN SHAPING. Take very light shear-scraping cuts with a gouge until only the centerline remains on a hemisphere. Work from center toward the edge of the chuck.

COMPLETE THE HEMISPHERE. Near the chuck, use a skew chisel as a scraper. The long point of the tool will let you reach under the rim of the chuck.

You can hear and feel when you have achieved a spherical shape, but it pays to get your fingers on the surface between the light shearing cuts. Stop the lathe frequently for a visual check. Near the chuck, I find that I have more control using a ¾-in. (19mm) skew chisel flat on the rest as a scraper (photo at left). The long point enables me to reach under the rim of the chuck. You've turned a hemisphere when you retain the pencil line but no flat sections. Sanding will further reduce the diameter, so you can retain a hint of the original flat on either side of the centerline. You can also check the development of the sphere using a ring (see p. 123), but this is not always as accurate as turning to the line.

6 Make a chuck to hold the hemisphere. The chuck needs to be marginally smaller than the diameter of the sphere, slightly tapered internally, and of course deep enough that the ball doesn't bottom out. Jam the half-completed sphere into the chuck, again aligning the centerline with the tail center.

7 Repeat step 5, again retaining the centerline with barely a flat section.

8 Sand the ball. Release it and rotate it in the chuck for sanding. Sand for only three or four seconds, then adjust the ball again to expose more of the unsanded face.

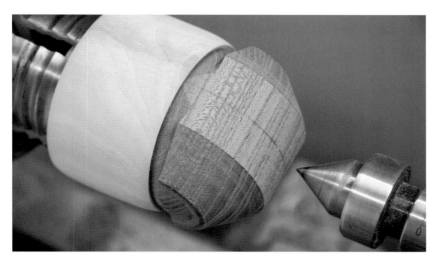

REVERSE THE SPHERE. Make a new jam chuck and press the completed hemisphere into it. Here, too, be sure to align the centerline with the tail center.

COME FULL CIRCLE. Finish shaping the sphere, using the same tools and techniques that you did for the first half.

GO LIGHTLY, KEEP MOVING. Avoid sanding one spot for more than a few seconds. Instead, continually reposition the sphere in the chuck to sand it uniformly. I used only 240-grit sandpaper to avoid removing too much material and distorting the sphere.

SPHERES ARE EASIER WITH A JIG

A sphere-cutting jig makes life much easier. The Vermec Sphere Cutting Jig I use has a cutter on the end of an adjustable arm that swings in an arc aligned with the centerline on the blank.

Begin by turning a cylinder with the same diameter as the ball you want to make. Mark a centerline against which to align the jig.

Turn the end to a hemisphere, keeping the centerline. To ensure the cleanest surface off the tool, the last two or three passes should be very light, working from the centerline toward the axis for a shear cut.

Use a parting tool to define the headstock side of the ball, then with a spindle gouge hog out the waste to create room for the jig. Use it to cut in as far as you can toward the chuck. Use a gouge or a skew chisel long-point-down to continue the curve. Mark the end of the jig-cut surface with a circle and part off the ball.

Press the spherical portion of the ball into a jam chuck. You want the ball skewed in the chuck, with the line marking the jig-cut portion as close as possible to the chuck rim. Turn away the waste until you retain only a hint of the circle.

Sand and finish the ball.

EASY DOES IT. As the hemisphere nears completion, make only very light passes with the cutter.

SPHERE-CUTTING JIG. A pin aligns the jig with the centerline. You then swing the cutter through an arc to define the hemisphere.

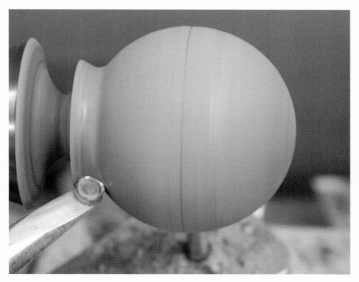

MAKE SPACE FOR THE JIG. Use a parting tool to define the other hemisphere, and a gouge to hog away waste near the chuck so there is space for the jig.

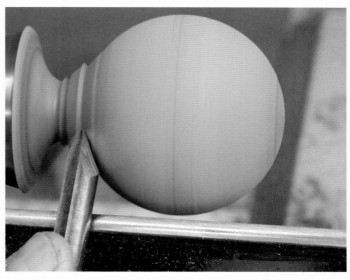

SWITCH TO HANDHELD TOOLS. You'll need to use a gouge or skew chisel to turn closer to center at the headstock end.

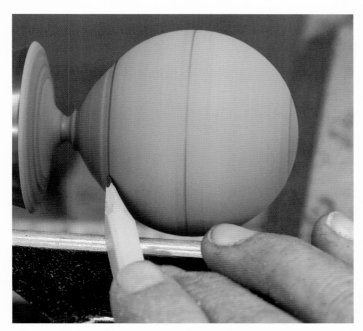

MARK THE END. Draw a circle where the jig's cut ended. This serves as a reference line as you complete the sphere.

RETURN TO THE JAM CHUCK. Press the sphere into a jam chuck, with the circle close to the chuck rim. Use a gouge to shear-scrape, then a skew chisel flat on the rest to complete the sphere, leaving only a hint of the pencilled circle.

FRUIT & VEGETABLES TO "CUT"

As kids, we learn by copying adults and want to get in on everything they do. For example, as soon as he could walk a neighbor's toddler would help his dad mow the front lawn with his own little plastic mower. He mimicked every move, every gesture. It was both hilarious and fascinating to watch.

For little helpers in the kitchen, you can turn all manner of ingredients. The fruits and vegetables you see here are split turnings, with Velcro® or magnets holding the halves together. The gap between halves is wide enough to insert a wooden knife and pry the pieces apart in a simulation of cutting. Once you've done a few tomatoes, apples, or pears, you can branch out into

KITCHEN PLAY-THINGS. Fruits and vegetables like these are easy to turn, and so is the knife that kids can use to "cut" the food.

cakes, muffins, hamburger buns, bread, eggs, and whatever else your imagination conjures up.

Rather than working to a drawing, you can use real fruit and vegetables as models. Keep in mind that you are turning stylized versions. These are round as they come off the lathe, of course, but with a bit of sanding and power-carving you can make them more realistic. The conical hole left by a tail center hints at the dimple on top of most fruits. Some simple whittling or sanding will easily accentuate this feature.

Although the individual pieces take a variety of shapes, this is fundamentally a centerwork project, with the grain parallel to the lathe axis. The turning, with skew chisels or gouges, is simple and quick. The greatest challenge is locating the magnets or Velcro that join the halves (see the sidebar on p. 108). I prefer magnets because they bring the parts together accurately time after time. Velcro is a much cheaper option, but it makes for a floppier and less accurate link.

In real life, we slice some fruit and vegetables from top to bottom (apples, pears, onions), and some across (carrots, zucchini, grapefruit). Never try to bandsaw one of these pieces in half once you've turned it—that's *really* dangerous. For anything you cut across, install the magnets or Velcro before the wood goes on the lathe, stick the blanks together, and mount them between centers. For anything sliced top to bottom, glue up a blank and split it after it is turned. Below, I take you through both procedures.

Turning Pieces Sliced Across

Epoxy magnets into the endgrain of a pair of blanks, and fix the assembly between centers. The magnets will keep the blanks together, but it helps to also have some non-slip cloth between the two to prevent slippage.

MAGNETS, NO SLIP. For fruit sliced across, fix magnets in the blanks before turning. Magnets keep pairs of blanks together on the lathe, but you need nonslip cloth between the blanks to prevent slippage (top). Here, I use a ¼-in. (6mm) spur drive. A larger drive means you have more to finish by hand or you need a longer blank.

FIXING MAGNETS AND VELCRO

The purpose of the magnets is to pull two halves together. If you put the magnets into the wood blanks the wrong way around they will repel each other. The two halves will never come together, which I'm sure would give many kids hours of amusement.

To ensure that pairs of magnets are correctly aligned, fit them joined in pairs. The rare earth magnets I use are ¼ in. (6mm) in diameter. I press them into a hole sized for them on top of a smear of 10-minute epoxy. Use a drill press to make the shallow hole for the magnet.

Because of the tight fit, you need a vent shaft to relieve the air pressure; I use the corner of a chisel to cut a tiny slit in each half. Press one magnet in position with the other attached, so you know the alignment is correct. Keep the top magnet attached as you find the hole on the other face. Squeeze the two halves together to seat the second magnet in its epoxy. Slide the halves apart, leaving each magnet in its own hole. If the magnet sits below the surface of the wood, sand back the face on a disk or belt sander until

DRILLING FOR MAGNETS. Rest the turning in a hole in a blank. This will support the piece and prevent it from slipping as you drill.

AIR VENT. Use the corner of a sharp chisel to create a tiny vent in the recess for the magnet.

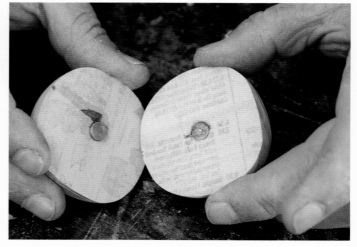

GLUE IN PAIRS. To keep the magnets oriented properly, stick them together. Put a dab of epoxy in both recesses and fit the magnets into one recess.

 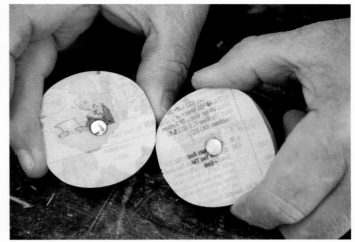

SQUEEZE. Push the two halves of the turning together, seating the second magnet in its recess (left). Then slide the halves apart (right).

the magnet is flush. Sparks tell you when you have sanded enough.

More economically, you can fix a magnet to one blank and a flathead steel nail or screw in the other. Drill a pilot hole for the nail or screw and add epoxy to the hole.

The process for fixing Velcro to the blanks is exactly the same as for magnets. The only difference is that the Velcro disks are set into a very shallow recess— merely the thickness of the adhesive on the Velcro. The hooks and loops sit proud of the cut face, so you don't need to chamfer the rims when finishing. The blanks go between centers on the lathe, with a ring of grip cloth around the Velcro to prevent the blanks from slipping.

To drill holes accurately for either magnets or Velcro, seat rounded parts in a hole, as the photos show.

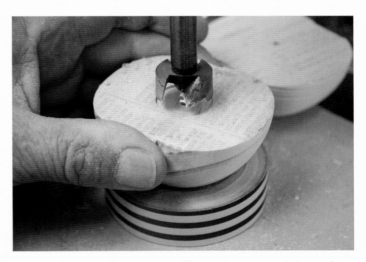

DRILLING FOR VELCRO. A self-adhesive Velcro disk needs a very shallow recess—just the thickness of the adhesive pad.

SAND A CHAMFER.
Run the rims across a sander to create an entry groove for the knife.

Use a skew chisel or gouge for the turning, then sand a slight chamfer around the rim on each half. This creates a gap for the wooden knife between the two halves.

To make a carrot like the one shown on p. 106, I used a three-part blank. To create its lumpy surface, raise and lower the bevel of the skew chisel as the cut proceeds. This produces a cleanly cut but ridged surface—something turners usually try to avoid, but it's just right here. When it came to the avocado, I used a Dremel® tool with a rounded burr to give the skin texture.

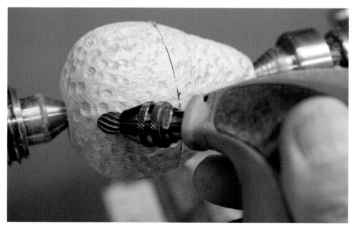

ADDING TEXTURE. To give a carrot its lumpy surface, raise and lower the bevel of the skew chisel as you move the tool along. A Dremel tool lets you mimic the rough skin of an avocado.

Turning Pieces Sliced End to End

For the turning, the joint will lie more or less parallel to the lathe axis, seen just above the shaving in the photo at right. This requires a laminated blank glued up with paper in the joint. Once you've finished the turning, you can easily wedge the halves apart with a chisel and attach the magnets.

With the halves separated, mark the face of each half so you can position the magnets exactly opposite one another. To mark where to drill for the magnets, tape a finish nail to one half, with the head positioned where you want the magnet. Align the two halves and press them together; the nail will dimple the wood. A light tap with a mallet will do the job if your grip isn't up to it.

TOP-TO-BOTTOM JOINT. The seam between the two halves of this emerging orange, visible just above the shaving coming off the chisel, is on the lathe axis.

PAPER JOINT. When you glue up the blanks, insert a piece of paper in the joint. When the turning is done, you can separate the halves cleanly with the tap of a chisel.

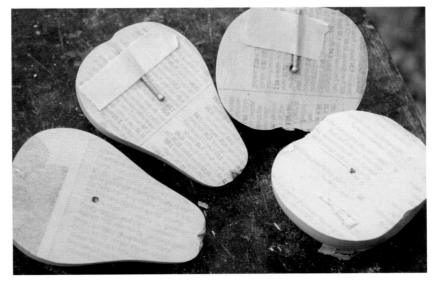

POSITIONING MAGNETS. Tape a finish nail to one half, then press the two halves together. The resulting dimple marks the center for the recess where the magnets will go.

SAND SMOOTH. If the two halves don't join cleanly, clean up the seam with a sander and chamfer the edges.

If the magnets end up slightly out of alignment, smooth out any variations or sharp edges with a pad sander held in a chuck on the lathe (photo above). Remember to chamfer the rims of each half to create a gap for the knife.

Shape the Knife

The knife is turned between centers. Then, off the lathe, you cut and sand one end to form the blade. When not used to "cut" fruit, a utensil like this makes an excellent pâté spreader or butter knife.

NOT JUST FOR YOUNGSTERS. Knives like these make good butter-spreaders as well as playthings. These are 5⅜ in. long by ⅝ in. thick (135mm by 17mm), made from mulberry.

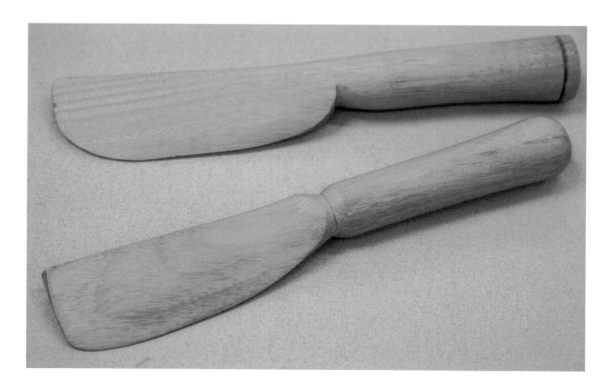

ROUGHED-OUT KNIFE. Prepare the knife blank at the bandsaw, removing some waste and tapering the end with the blade. Just be sure to leave the handle end square.

Begin with a blank about 6 in. (150mm) long and ¾ in. (20mm) square at the handle end. The blade end can be thinner and wider; it's fine to start with a wedge-shaped blank, provided it is square at the handle end, as shown in the photo above.

1 Rough out the handle using a skew chisel flat on the rest to peel about half the blank to a cylinder.

2 Use planing cuts to finish the handle and shape the profile of the edge of the knife blade. There will not be much wood coming around as you define the cutting edge and possibly the top. Sand and polish the handle at this stage.

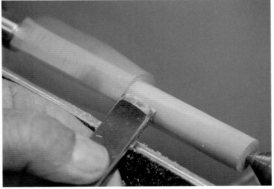

HANDLE FIRST. Take peeling cuts with a skew chisel to begin rounding the handle.

ROUGHED-OUT BLADE. Take planing cuts to finish the handle and begin shaping the blade.

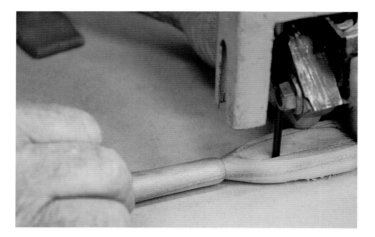

3 On the bandsaw, shape the knife blade. The idea is to cut a flat surface at right angles to the knife blade, then stand the knife on that surface as you cut facets either side of a centerline.

4 Use a soft sanding pad for the final shaping of the blade. Don't make the cutting edge sharp. An 80-grit abrasive disk will remove the bulk of the waste in a few seconds. Contrary to standard practice, I find I can jump straight to 240-grit to complete the job in a few more seconds.

BANDSAW THE BLADE. Begin by cutting a flat surface at right angles to the blade (top). Then, with the knife resting on that edge, trim away waste (above). For safety's sake, use a sharp blade and pull the wood through the saw with your fingers safely behind the blade.

NOT TOO SHARP. Refine the blade shape at the sander, making sure to keep the cutting edge blunt.

CROQUET SET

C roquet is a wonderful game that requires considerable skill, cunning, and deviousness. It's rather like billiards, only on a grand scale, played outdoors on grass. Each player has a colored ball (so they know which one is theirs) and a mallet.

The aim is to hit the ball through a sequence of hoops (known as wickets in the United States), ending at a post. Players earn points for going through a hoop, hitting the post, and also for hitting other players' balls. There are national croquet organizations and the World Croquet

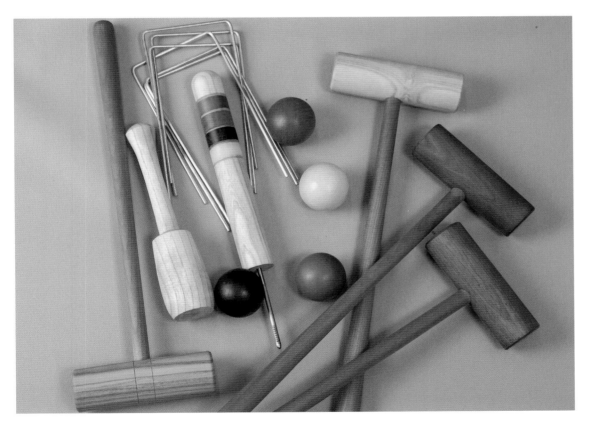

A FULL SET. I made this junior croquet set for 6- to 8-year-olds. The mallet handles are 20 in. (510mm) long; the heads are 6 in. (150mm) long and 2 in. (50mm) in diameter. The balls are 2⅜ in. (60mm) in diameter. Between the balls are the finish post and a carver's mallet to thump both it and the hoops into the ground.

Federation, which publish formal rules and sanction versions of the game, all of which you can find on the Internet. Played informally in backyards and gardens, croquet seems to have as many variations as there are families playing the game. If you have no hoops, then play a variation of lawn bowls, seeing how close you can hit your ball to a target ball. Or aim at empty tin cans, or set up a sort of mini-golf course. Kids will soon make up their own game and rules.

Turning a mallet and the posts is fairly straightforward; turning the balls can be tricky. Fortunately, as I explained in the chapter on spheres (p. 98), you can use a sphere-cutting jig to take much of the nervous strain out of the job. The techniques required for the mallet are pretty well covered in Chapter 5. However there are a few tips to help you with the mallet, along with a few design considerations.

MALLET

Croquet mallets come in a range of sizes, so the dimensions will depend on the height of the potential users. As a rule of thumb, a mallet stood on end should reach to the top of your leg, where it joins the pelvis.

At the top end of the sport, competition mallets have handles about 36 in. (915mm) long, turned from a 1³⁄₈-in. (35mm) square blank; the heads are about 3¹⁄₈ in. by 9 in. (80mm by 230mm). Junior mallets, designed for 10-year-olds, typically have handles about 26 in. (660mm) long, with heads 2³⁄₄ in. by 8 in. (70mm by 200mm). The mallets you see in the sequence below are for a couple of younger and smaller children.

BALLS

The standard size for a croquet ball is 3⁵⁄₈ in. (92mm) in diameter, with a weight of about a pound. But as with mallets, there are variations. If you're making a croquet set for smaller kids, reduce the size of the balls accordingly.

HOOPS

Tournament hoops are only marginally wider than the balls that go through them, and they are made of iron bar ⁵⁄₈ in. (16mm) in diameter. For a backyard game played for fun by young novices, hoops can be wider and less substantial. (If you own welding gear, of course, you can make the real thing.) The hoops in the set

CENTERED. To keep the hole for the handle centered on the mallet head, measure and mark identical lengths from either side of the hole.

shown on p. 115 were bent from 2-ft. (610mm) lengths of ⁵⁄₃₂-in.-diameter (4mm) steel irrigation riser rods. To shape a hoop, I put the rod in a vise and pulled the ends around. The hoops are slightly wider than the 4-in. (100mm) vise jaws. That's way larger than they need to be, but a bigger target for young players using smaller balls is not a bad thing.

Turn the Mallet Head

The blanks for the mallet heads shown on p. 115 were 2³⁄₈ in. square and 8 in. long (60mm by 200mm). That yielded a final diameter of 2¹⁄₈ in. (55mm) and a length of 6 in. (150mm).

1 Drill a ³⁄₄-in.-diameter (19mm) hole for the handle in the middle of one side of a squared blank. Stop short of drilling completely through. It's essential that the lathe axis passes through the middle of the hole once the blank is on the lathe. Find center on each end of the blank by drawing the diagonals; be sure you locate the drive and tail center cones spot on where the diagonals cross.

2 Turn a cylinder to size using calipers and a skew chisel. Lay out the length of the blank, measuring from each side of the hole so that it will be centered on the mallet head (photo on the facing page).

3 Turn the two ends flat using a gouge or skew chisel, as shown on pp. 28 and 29. If need be, trim either end to ensure that the hole for the handle is centered.

4 Chamfer the rim at each end to help prevent the mallet head from splitting in use.

5 Sand and finish everything you can reach. As usual, I apply boiled linseed oil liberally with the lathe off, then a layer of beeswax over the top with the lathe running.

SPLIT PREVENTER. A chamfer will help prevent the sides of the mallet from splintering when it hits the balls.

SMOOTH AND FLAT. Use the miter gauge on a disk sander to ensure that the ends of the mallet head are flat and square to the body. A soft sanding pad in the lathe also works well for cleaning up the center nub.

6 Saw off the nubs at either end and sand the ends smooth. I find a small resilient sanding pad ideal. A good alternative is to use the miter gauge on a disk sander, which also keeps the end dead flat (see the photo above).

SUPPORT THE CUT.
To prevent the handle
from whipping, use
your free hand to sup-
port it as well as to
guide the tool across
the wood.

Turn the Mallet Handle

I made the mallet shown here with a 6-year-old
and an 8-year-old in mind. The blank is 20 in.
long and 1³⁄₁₆-in. square (510mm by 30mm).
Blanks this length can be safely run at 1,800 rpm.
Whipping can be a problem at higher speeds,
however, especially if the tailstock is wound in
tight enough to bow the blank. Start at around
1,400 rpm, or slower with longer blanks.

These Mallets Aren't Hammers

Croquet mallets are not built for pounding the post
into the ground—or anything else. You'll need a separate mallet like the carver's mallet included in the
group photo at the beginning of this chapter. One of
those is easy to turn in a few minutes.

1 Turn the square blank to round. To minimize whipping, tighten the tail center when
you start the lathe, then back it off a fraction.
You'll hear the lathe give a sort of sigh as the
pressure is relieved. Remember, you want the
tail center to support the end of the blank, not
push hard against it. Slender spindles squeezed
between centers tend to bow. Also, support the
wood with your free hand, equalizing any tool
pressure against the wood so it runs true.

2 With the corners gone, establish the diameter to fit into the hole in the mallet head.
In the top left photo on the facing page I'm
using a ¾-in. (19mm) spur drive; it is the same
size as the hole, so I can use the drive as a gauge
in addition to my wooden gauge. I sand away the
waste at the end of the handle and chamfer it on
the disk sander so I can test the fit. Rotate the
head on the handle to develop a burnish mark,
and use that as a guide as you extend the
amount that will fit onto the handle. When
you're almost down to the right size, switch to
sandpaper so you don't make the end too small.

TWO SIZE GAUGES. If the spur drive is the same diameter as the hole in the mallet head, you can use the drive to help gauge the size you need. But a wooden template is more accurate.

CHAMFER AND BURNISH. Chamfer the end of the handle to make it easy to insert into its hole.

TURN TO THE MARK. Take very light cuts to pare the handle down to the burnish mark resulting from the test fit.

GO EASY. Spiral marks like these tell you that you're applying too much pressure against the axis with the tool. Let the wood come to the tool.

STEADY. A three-point steady rest stabilizes the turning. It's another way to prevent chatter marks.

3 Turn and finish the rest of the handle using the skew chisel and grips shown on pp. 33 and 38. Spiral chatter marks like those shown at center right are a sign that there was too much tool pressure against the wood. To minimize chatter when turning very long and slender spindles, try a lower speed—1,000 rpm, say—rather than higher. Another common solution is to use a three-point steady rest. The rollers tend to burnish the wood but the mark sands away in a millisecond. Of course, if the spiral chatter is bad enough to keep as a decorative feature, forget the sanding.

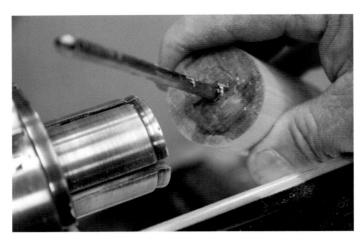

SAVE YOUR LAWN. A long spike or a piece of steel rod will hold the finish post in place without leaving a large hole in the lawn. Grind the end of the metal to a blunt point.

DRILL THE POST. Fix a drill bit in the headstock and center it in the hole left by the tail center. Grip the post with one hand, turn on the lathe, and advance the tailstock.

Turn the Post

You can turn a post with a point to drive into the ground, but it will make a big hole in your lawn. Less invasive is a steel rod, like the 6-in. (150mm) nail shown here, epoxied into the bottom of the post.

1 Drill a hole for the nail in one end of a 1½ in. (38mm) cylinder. This is easily done on the lathe with a drill mounted in pin jaws or a drill chuck. With the lathe off, mount the cylinder between the drill and the tail center. Position the drill in the hole left by the tail center when you roughed the blank to size. Then turn on the lathe and hold the blank while you advance the tailstock.

2 Epoxy the nail in place. When the adhesive has cured, grind the nail head to a blunt point.

3 Turn the post with the rod held in a chuck. True up the endgrain, taking the cut right to the nail. Use abrasive to remove any epoxy from the metal. Then give the post a rounded top, which makes it less likely to split when you knock it into the ground.

4 Turn the five grooves that separate the colors and paint the rings while the post is on the lathe. You can sharply define the painted edges by cutting the grooves again after the paint has dried. This also removes any paint that got into a groove.

FINISH THE END. Hold the spike in the headstock and clean up the end of the post (left). Sand away any excess epoxy (right).

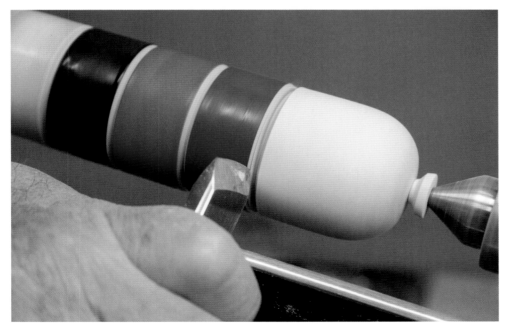

PAINT AND TRIM. Turn five grooves and paint the colored bands in between them. When the paint is dry, re-cut the grooves to define the bands crisply.

TEETHER & RATTLE

These two projects use the same turning technique: Both are gripped at one end while the other end hurtles around in space, threatening to whack your fingers if you get them too close. The teether is for infants to chew to toughen their gums, and the rattle is to, well, rattle. And probably chew as well.

When teething, babies have a natural inclination to gnaw on anything that fits in their mouths. The favorite chew of one baby boy I knew was the beaded end of one of my spatulas—

FOR INFANTS AND TODDLERS. Teethers and rattles to wave around and chew. These are turned from pear, oak, and ash. Pear is a woodturner's dream—tight-grained and quite hard, yet wonderful to work.

LAY OUT THE SPHERES. Use a shopmade gauge and a ruler to mark the cylinder for the ends and midpoints of the spheres at the ends of the dumbbell.

his mother soon asked me to make another so she still had something to stir his porridge with.

For either the rattle or the teether, you'll need a blank about 1½ in. (38mm) square and about 4½ in. (115mm) long. The finished items will be about 4 in. (100mm) long.

Turn a Teether

The teether starts as a blank that is turned between centers into a dumbbell. Each end is then chucked and re-chucked—five different fixings in all, four of them in a chuck with one jaw missing. In a pinch you might consider making a jam-fit wooden chuck with a hole for the handle, but a mechanical chuck is much easier and safer; it demands less accuracy and gives a better grip. Any chuck marks are easily removed at the finishing stage. You end up with rings that are 90 degrees to each other.

1 Size the blank to a cylinder that your chuck jaws can close on. Mark the blank with guidelines for the two spherical ends. The one shown above is 1⁹⁄₁₆ in. (40mm) in diameter to fit my Vicmarc Shark Jaws.

2 Turn the first sphere using the techniques detailed in the chapter on spheres, p. 98. For this project, though, true spheres are not essential, and they don't even need to be exactly the same size. Try turning by eye, checking your progress by running something round and hollow over the surface. The photo below shows a brass ferrule, although anything round and pipe-like will do.

Use a spindle gouge to shape the handle before starting the second sphere. The handle needs to end up at about ½ in. (15mm) in diameter. As usual, when you've turned and sanded

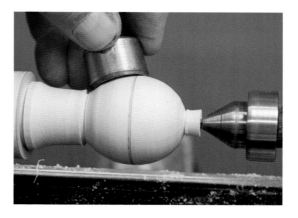

SPHERE-TESTING. A gap beneath the ring tells me I have more wood to remove.

THE HANDLE COMES NEXT. With the first sphere done, cut the handle down to size and turn the second sphere.

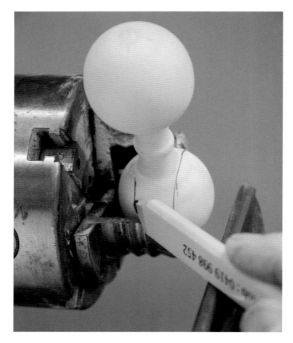

IDEAL CHUCKING. Long-reach jaws like these Shark jaws are well-suited for holding a sphere to be flattened. Here, I'm using the width of the handle as a guide when marking the sphere to show how much wood to remove.

the barbells and parted off, you'll need to saw away and sand the nubs on each end before proceeding.

3 Transform one sphere into a flat, hollow ring. You can accomplish this in one of three ways:

Use jaws with a long reach. My long Shark jaws, shown in the bottom photo at left, are nearly ideal for this turning. One jaw is removed.

Use pin jaws. If you don't have long Shark jaws, a set of pin jaws is a good substitute. In order to work, the jaws need to grip the full diameter of the sphere. All four jaws stay on the chuck.

Use a sander. If your chuck has only standard or short jaws, flatten the spheres on a sander so they can seat in the chuck.

If you can use a chuck for this step and are not using pin jaws, remove one of the jaws to make room for the handle. Keep the handle perpendicular to the lathe axis. Grip one sphere in the chuck; the other will spin around like a satellite. Spin the work by hand to be sure that nothing hits the tool rest.

With the lathe running at about 1,700 rpm, use a ¼-in. (6mm) bowl gouge to flatten the hemisphere and then hollow it. Be sure to keep your hand on the tailstock side of the tool rest, to avoid injury from the satellite sphere as it whips around (see the top left photo on the facing page).

As you hollow through to the other hemisphere, you may find that a ½-in. (12mm) round-nose scraper is more effective and easier to use. Sand the inner lip before re-chucking this end.

MIND THE SATELLITE. When hollowing a sphere, keep the tool rest between your fingers and the spinning wood to keep them from being whacked.

4 Reverse the hemisphere in the chuck and complete the ring. Use the same gouge and scraper to repeat the cuts on the other side.

5 Repeat steps 3 and 4 on the other hemisphere so that this ring is set at 90 degrees to the first.

SCRAPE THE HOLLOW. Switch from a gouge to a round-nose scraper as the depth of the hollow increases. The scraper is easier to control.

RE-CHUCK. Reverse the piece in the chuck. Try to orient it so that the sides of the ring will be parallel. Use a gouge and scraper to complete the ring.

6 Sand the outside, removing chuck marks and softening edges. Use a sanding pad on the lathe, and do hand-sanding either with a spongy backing or by rasping with a length of abrasive.

FOUR WAYS TO SAND. A sanding pad on the lathe smooths the outside of the ring (above). Hand-sanding with the abrasive wrapped around a soft backing also works. Or pull lengths of abrasive across the ring or weave it in and out and pull back and forth (left).

SECOND THOUGHT. After sanding this teether smooth, I went back to the sanding pad to make facets on the surface for a more stimulating chew.

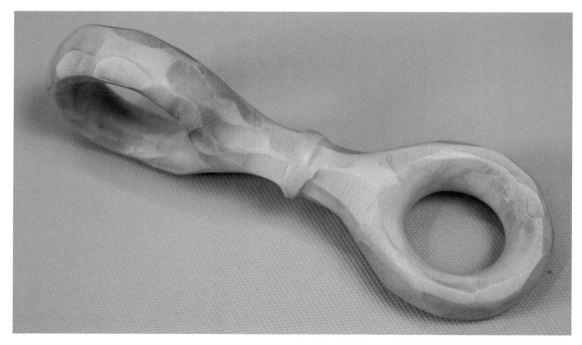

ANOTHER APPROACH: DRILL THE SPHERES

As an alternative to hollowing the spheres on the lathe, you can use a drill press to create the rings. You will drill through the spheres, so use some scrap MDF or plywood, drilled with a couple of holes, to protect the drill-press table and to support the work. As the left photo below shows, the end with my finger is in the first supporting hole. The pencilled cross shows where I need to drill, so when this point is beneath the drill bit, I clamp the MDF in position, fixing the first hole in position. Next, I remove the barbell and drill a second support hole. These two holes keep the barbell horizontal and firmly in position for drilling.

The spheres can then be flattened on a sander. The flattened spheres now go into a chuck so you can true

the holes and sand the rims, or you can forget more turning and detail the rims using a small sander.

If you don't own a drill press or a large enough drill, simply flatten the spheres for what should be a good chew.

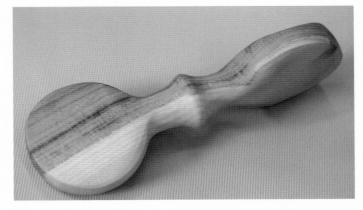

STILL A GOOD CHEW. Simple flattened spheres are easy to make with a disk sander and will still please an infant.

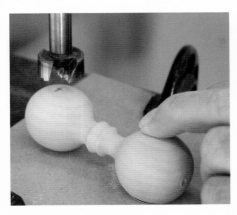

DRILL FOR SUPPORT. Holes in a piece of scrap MDF will support the work as you drill out the spheres. Here, my finger holds one sphere in a support hole as I align the bit over the mark for the hole in the other sphere. With everything aligned, I clamp the scrap in position and drill a second support hole.

DRILL THE SPHERES. Hold the teether in the support holes and drill one sphere. Then flip the piece end for end to drill the other sphere. Be sure to rotate the teether before drilling the second hole so the rings are at 90 degrees to each other.

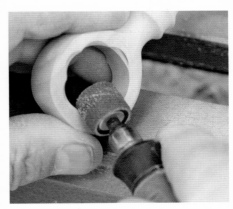

SAND AND DETAIL. Flatten the rings on a disk sander. You can add detail with a small sanding drum in a Dremel tool, as shown.

SPLIT THE BLANK.
A good blow to a wide chisel will split the wood cleanly. But be sure to align the chisel with the medullary rays, not the growth rings.

Turn a Rattle

This is a nifty little project that will impress adults more than any child because, despite the rattle rattling, the object appears to be made from one solid piece of wood. The trick is to split the blank, do a bit of hollowing, then glue it back together for turning. You'll get the best results by using a wood that splits easily like ash, oak, or most other woods with strong medullary rays. If possible, use a blank that is quartersawn.

1 You need a blank about 1⁹⁄₁₆ in. (40mm) square and about 4½ in. (115mm) long. Cleave the blank in two, and try not to touch the cleaved surfaces because you want them to go back together exactly as they parted. The blank needs to be split on the radius, parallel to the medullary rays rather than with the growth rings.

IMPOSSIBLE. Rattles like these appear to be made from a solid piece of wood. In fact, they are turned from a single piece that's split and then rejoined. The glue line is invisible on the oak rattle (left) and barely discernible on the other two.

HOLLOW ONE HALF. Use long-reach or pin jaws to hold the wood while you turn a hollow. A scraper will do the job with little risk of a catch or kickback.

2 Remove one jaw from a chuck and mount one half of the blank. Seat it at the base of the jaws with the end hard against the center jaw. Turn a hemisphere into the blank, leaving about ³⁄₁₆ in. (5mm) thickness in the base.

3 Mount the matching end of the other half of the blank in the chuck and turn a hemisphere to match the first. An exact match isn't necessary because nobody will see how the two hollows fit together, but for reassembly you need at least ³⁄₁₆ in. (5mm) of wood all around the hollow.

4 Mark the edge of the hole on the outside of the blank. Drop in a noisemaker, like the screw shown in the photo at right, fit the two pieces together, and do a test-shake. You can try all manner of seeds and pebbles or nuts and bolts before gluing the blank together.

5 Reassemble the blank, taking care to align it exactly. Ten-minute epoxy keeps this blank together, but any good-quality wood glue should do the job. You don't want the join to fail, releasing the rattling bit to be swallowed.

TEST RUN. Dry-fit the pieces with a noisemaker inside. Give it a shake to hear how it sounds. Mark the edge of the hollow to guide you when turning the outside of the rattle.

PART AND SHAPE. Make a parting cut to define the end of the rattle. The cut is to the left of the mark showing where the interior hollow ends. Shape the end before starting the handle.

PEEL AND SHEAR. Take peeling cuts with a skew chisel (as shown) to bring the handle down to the desired diameter. Then finish the shaping with a series of shear cuts.

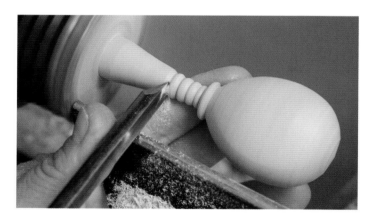

GETTING FANCY. Try dressing up the handle with a series of beads. Reach under the tool rest to support the work with your fingers and use your thumb to guide the gouge.

6 Put the blank on the lathe between centers or hold it in a chuck and turn it into a rattle. First, make a parting cut to define the head. Always mark the exact depth of the inside so you know precisely where it is; the parting cut is ³/₁₆ in. (5mm) to the left of the depth mark. Finish turning the head before starting on the handle.

Use a skew chisel to shape the handle, first flat on the rest for a series of peeling cuts, then for shear cuts.

If you want to go fancy on the handle, try turning a set of beads with a detail gouge.

Sand and finish the rattle before parting off. I use my usual mix of oil and beeswax. Both teether and rattle are going to need washing, and this is a finish that will come off in hot water and detergent. The wood can be refurbished with a small amount of vegetable, olive, or nut oil (checking for allergies if using the last). Or simply leave the wood plain. It might be tastier that way.

NESTING TUBS

Stacking and unstacking a nest of tubs can keep toddlers occupied for hours as they begin to understand size differences and refine their ability to put things exactly where they want. Making each tub in the set a different color means older kids and adults can offer advice about which one goes where and teach colors at the same time. ("Won't it fit? Try the yellow one.")

When these tubs have served their original purpose, they can be used as handy little cylindrical bowls for all sorts of stuff: keys, elastic bands, loose change, and the like. They should last a lifetime.

STACK OR NEST.
These cylindrical vessels fit inside one another or can be made into a tower.

Choose the Right Wood

Tubs are just cylindrical bowls, so any small bowl blank is suitable, provided it is free of splits. The blanks for the nests shown here were sawn from offcuts I had squirreled away on drafty open shelves, where they could air-dry over several years. If you have a variety of blanks, each tub in a set can be a different wood.

You will get the best results with wood known for its stability, like walnut, cherry, or ash. If the wood shrinks or swells too much with changes in temperature and humidity, the tubs won't nest properly. It's a good idea to part-turn a tub blank, as you might rough out a bowl to speed seasoning. Removing the center releases tension in the wood, often causing a form to warp over a couple of days. After that, you can remount the piece on the lathe, true it, and finish it.

The grain for the tub blanks can be aligned either across or in line with the lathe axis. I tend to favor cross-grain pieces, partly for their more attractive grain patterns, but mainly for their superior strength. Those qualities overwhelm the downside of cutting endgrain cleanly twice on the inside and twice on the outside. A finished endgrain tub with walls less than ⅛ in. (3mm) thick will be fairly stable but fragile compared to a cross-grain version, and too easily split.

When you make nesting tubs, finish the smallest one first. You can then fit it into the next one up, making sure the rims are level. Take great care with the smallest in a set, making sure it's cylindrical on the outside. The inside can be slightly wider at the bottom. The walls and base need to be at least ⅛ in. (3mm) thick, with about ³⁄₃₂ in. (2.5mm) of clearance between tubs. The ones you see in the photos range from about 2⅛ in. (55mm) to slightly more than 4 in. (100 mm) in diameter.

GRADUATED. The tubs in this set range in diameter from 2⅛ in. to 4 in. (55mm to 100mm), and in height from 1⅛ in to 2⅛ in. (30mm to 55mm).

START SMALL. Make the smallest tub first, holding it on a screw chuck as you turn it to a cylinder.

SHAPE THE TENON. Use a square-end scraper to true the face, leaving a tenon. Then use a spindle gouge (as shown) to dovetail the tenon a few degrees.

COMPLETE THE OUTSIDE. Use a gouge to bring the outside to its final size.

SMOOTH FINISH. Shear scraping with a skewed scraper will produce the smoothest surface on endgrain.

The height is about half the diameter. Having made the smallest, you can then find a blank for the next one up until you run out of material. There's no reason you can't have tubs large enough for a toddler to sit in. No matter what their size, each tub is made in the same way.

How to Turn a Cross-Grain Tub

1 Mount a blank for the smallest tub in the set on a screw chuck. True it, using a gouge to cut in from either face. Then use a ¾-in. (19mm) square-end scraper to true the base, leaving a short tenon that fits your chuck. Dovetail the tenon about 2 degrees by easing the nose of a spindle gouge into the corner at the bottom of the tenon. Keep the tool on its side, with the bevel rubbing the wood.

2 Grip the blank by the tenon and true the face. Next, complete the outside before you hollow the tub, using a gouge to turn the profile to size and calipers to ensure you turn a cylinder. The best surface will often come from shear-scraping, using a skewed scraper tilted up on its side. Keep the cut in the lower half of the tool's edge.

DEPTH HOLE. Hold a drill bit against the tub to see how deep to make the hole. Use your thumb as a depth gauge for drilling.

A Simple Depth Gauge

A handy way to keep track of where the tool is in relation to the bottom of the tub is to pop a rare earth magnet on the tool blade.

3 To begin the hollowing, use a depth hole to tell you how far down to hollow. I use a standard ¼-in. (6mm) drill bit in a shopmade handle. Use your thumb to mark the depth you want to drill, then push the drill into the hole left by the screw chuck until your thumb meets the wood. Do this in a series of short jabs to keep the bit from heating up too much, and clear the shavings after each jab.

You can hollow with a small bowl gouge, but it's much faster to use a scraper, working from the center outward. The depth hole makes hollowing easier because it provides clearance for the first cut. When using a scraper to hollow a cylinder, set the tool rest at about center height so only the top left corner and side of the tool blade can contact the wood. If the rest is low, the lower left side of the tool will contact the wood, forcing the edge toward the center as the

HOLLOW WITH A SCRAPER. Work from the center outward to hollow the tub. Use about two-thirds of the scraper's edge at one time. Here, I'm midway through a second cut.

CHECK FOR UNIFORMITY. Calipers will tell you if the inside is cylindrical or if there are spots that need to be removed.

cut proceeds, creating a wall that's thicker at its base.

Before making the final cut, stop the lathe and use calipers to ensure the inside is cylindrical. It doesn't matter if the hollow is slightly wider at the bottom, provided the rim is the right thickness.

A gouge will produce the cleanest finishing cut. Use a spindle gouge (rather than a bowl gouge), starting the tool on its side. The shavings will usually obscure your view of the edge, making it easy to cut into the base. So stop the cut midway to clear the shavings and check your progress. Clean out the corner with a square-end scraper, and use a mini-straightedge like the end of a metal ruler to check that the bottom is flat.

Sand everything you can reach. Now is also a good time to color the wood.

FINISHING CUT. A gouge on its side will give you the smoothest finish on the inside wall. Use a scraper in the corner to achieve a crisp angle between bottom and side.

REVERSE CHUCK.
Expand the chuck jaws inside the tub so you can turn away the tenon. Non-slip fabric protects the wood.

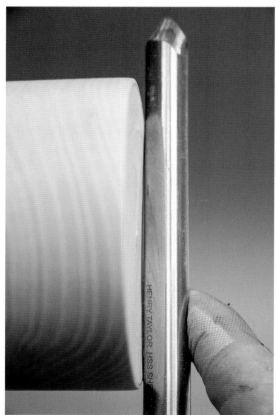

TENON REMOVAL. You can shear cut from the outside toward the center with a gouge. However, I prefer to shear scrape from the center outward (above); this is a more controlled cut. Use the gouge to see if the face is slightly concave (right).

4 Remove the tenon from the bottom. Reverse the tub over the chuck jaws. I rarely bother, but if you're worried about chuck marks, wrap a couple of layers of non-slip cloth around the jaws to protect the wood (see the top photo on the facing page). You can turn away the tenon using a spindle gouge for a shear cut with the bevel rubbing, although I usually prefer to start with a less aggressive shear-scrape with the gouge rolled on its side and the flute facing the wood being cut. Make sure the bottom is slightly concave, so the tub sits on the rim of its base; you can use the gouge as a handy straightedge.

5 Repeat steps 1 through 3 to shape the next-largest tub in the set, hollowing until the smaller tub fits inside and both rims are level. If you hollow too deep, fit the smaller tub inside and mark its height (see the photo at right). Remove the smaller tub and turn the rim down

MATCHING RIMS. Use the smaller tub to mark the larger one, showing how much to cut away so the tubs are a uniform height.

SMALL CUTS. Reduce the height of the tub with a gouge, taking small arcing cuts to keep the inside edge intact.

SHORTENING AN ENDGRAIN TUB. Use a skew chisel to cut away a ring of waste (left). Go gently, then use the skew bevel side (right) to clean up the end.

to the line, using the nose of a gouge to make small arcing cuts that sweep toward center (see the bottom photo on p. 137). Don't use a scraper; if you inadvertently take a slightly heavy cut, you can shatter the rim or even the entire tub. If the wall of the larger tub looks too thick in relation to the smaller tub, now it's the time to slim it with more of the shear-scraping cuts described in step 3.

Once you have finished shaping the larger tub, reverse it on the chuck to remove the tenon. Continue making larger tubs until your set is complete.

How to Turn an Endgrain Tub

The steps for turning an endgrain tub are the same as for cross-grain. Hold the blank in a chuck, but use a skew chisel to shape the profile. Hollowing is still easiest with a square-end scraper, but when it comes to trimming the rim, you need to take a different approach because of the grain direction. If you need to remove more than $1/32$ in. (1mm) of wood, use the long point of a skew chisel to cut off a ring to avoid splintering the endgrain on the inner lip (left photo above). Then ease the bevel side of the skew against the endgrain to remove the remaining waste (right photo above).

GOBLET

I am reliably informed that no young wizard with a wand can operate efficiently without a goblet, so here's one made to look mystical, ancient, and magical. It's a repository of spells and a vessel from which to swig magic potions. Highly polished, flashy wood isn't the go here. The cup should look as if it's been around the block a few times and seen a bit of life. It's of a size that requires two hands.

You can turn the goblet with one fixing, holding it at the base in a chuck. Once turned, you can use carving chisels or a Dremel tool to add whatever embellishments you fancy.

1 Begin with a blank about 5 in. (127mm) square and twice as long, with the grain running the length of the blank. With the lathe running at about 900 rpm, turn a cylinder with a tenon to fit your chuck. The jaws need to dig in on a wide diameter and butt up against the shoulder on the blank (as shown in the top photo on p. 140). Remember to true the cylinder once it's in the chuck, so that you can tell in an instant if it is pulled off-center as work proceeds.

2 Complete the inside before tackling the outside. This allows you to retain as much thickness around the inside shape as possible while it's being hollowed. Aim for a wall thickness of about ½ in. (13mm) at the thinnest point so you can carve into the profile later.

CREATIVE POSSIBILITIES. Goblets like these give you ample opportunities to practice your carving and embellishing skills.

SQUARE UP. When you turn a long blank, you want the chuck jaws to butt up against the tenon shoulder for the most secure grip. Here, the tenon is about 1 in. (25mm) long, held in 3¼ in. (83mm) Shark jaws.

STARTER HOLE. To make it easier to hollow the goblet, drill a starter hole in the end. Use a handheld depth drill, as shown here, or a drill mounted in a chuck in the tailstock.

Begin by drilling a depth hole a little less than half the length of the cylinder. If you're nervous about using a depth drill, mount a drill in the tailstock and wind it in. The hand-held depth drill is quick and easy; drilling from the tailstock allows you to make a larger hole using a Forstner bit. A depth hole makes the initial cuts a lot easier than going into solid endgrain.

I begin hollowing with a ¾-in. (20mm) scraper that is ⅜ in. (9mm) thick, with a round nose ground with a longer left-side edge. The cut should produce the spurt of dust and small shavings shown on the nose of the tool in the top photo on the facing page.

Use only a small part of the edge at one time. Plant your left hand on the rest and use your thumb as a lateral fulcrum for the tool. You can ease the tool forward with your thumb, at the same time swinging the edge through an arc toward the center. You can also start the cut at the center and swing the edge toward the rim, but any outward force against the wood can pull the blank off-center; when that happens, stop the lathe immediately and re-center the blank in the chuck, truing it if necessary. Throughout the hollowing process, try to keep your left hand on top of the cylinder to equalize tool pressure against the wood. Remember you're trying to let the wood come to the tool, rather than pushing the tool into the wood. As you deepen the hole, keep the cuts as near parallel to the lathe axis as you can, and direct any force toward the headstock.

When cutting more than 2 in. (50mm) over the rest, I opt for a heavier 1⅜-in. by ⅜-in. (35mm by 9mm) scraper with a 24-in.-long (610mm) handle. (As a rule of thumb, the tool's handle should be four to five times the length you are working over the rest.) I keep the handle under my forearm or against my side and my hand over the ferrule.

When you have turned the inside of the goblet, sand it so you have a fixed surface to which you can relate the outside surface.

SCRAPE THE CUP. Use a scraper with an asymmetrical round-nose grind for the hollowing. Your left thumb serves as a fulcrum to swing the tool in an arc, and your fingers steady the blank.

LARGER TOOL, LESS VIBRATION. As you hollow deeper, switch to a larger scraper with a longer handle, and steady it with your forearm. This helps minimize the chatter that results when a tool is extended far over the rest.

3 Measure the internal depth and mark it on the outside. Then part in to begin shaping the outside of the cup. Make the parting cut to the left of the depth mark, leaving some extra material for the base of the cup. If you mark the exact depth, you'll know exactly where the inside is. Shape the profile of the cup, working up to the left side of the parting cut. Don't remove any wood on the left side of the parting cut, lest you lose track of where the inside is.

4 This being a ceremonial sort of goblet, I leave a wide raised area for later decoration and define it with a couple of grooves; then, with the skew chisel flat on the tool rest, I peel away the waste on either side. You can slide the long point into the endgrain and get a very clean surface. If the skew edge is slightly radiused, the trailing part of the edge won't mess up the bit you've just cut.

With the raised area done, begin cutting the outer curve using the skew's short corner. Then, about halfway down, turn the tool over to finish the curve with the long point. This technique has two advantages: One, you barely have to move your hands or your body; two, you can see what you're doing. Keep the edge clear of the wood and you'll avoid a catch. Remember it's only the bevel side rubbing the wood, and you're cutting with the point.

DEFINE THE CUP. Mark the depth of the hollowed cup and make a deep parting cut slightly to the left of that mark to begin defining the goblet's shape.

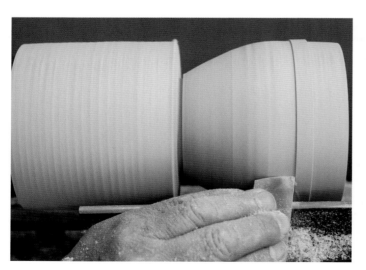

SPACE FOR DECORATION. You can embellish the goblet any way you please. I like to use a skew chisel to make a wide band, or frieze, near the lip for some carving.

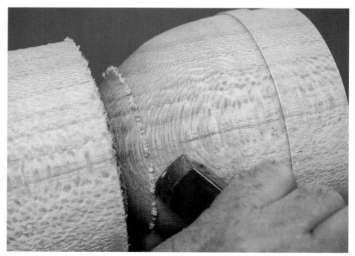

SHAPE THE CUP. Begin cutting the final shape with the short corner of a skew chisel. Then, halfway down, flip the tool over to finish the cut with the long point, as shown here.

5 Embellish the profile. The wall is thick enough, at ½ in. (13mm), that you can sand or turn away decorations you don't like and begin again. I begin by carving a series of marks on the wide raised area, working fast and loose and by eye with a Dremel tool, pivoting it on the tool rest.

Next, a series of coves breaks up the surface below the bead. For a cleanly shaped cove, cut in from either side. The ⅜-in. (9mm) spindle gouge will want to catch, so I hold the tool very firmly as I ease it into the wood with my thumb. For a really secure grip, I hook my forefinger under the rest so I can pull the tool hard onto it. The edge of the cut is not that clean, but burning or sanding will soon fix that.

6 Complete the stem and base with a ½-in. (13mm) spindle gouge. Part in to the diameter of the chuck jaws to define the base.

ADD SOME CARVING. Here, I'm using a Dremel tool to quickly carve some marks on the wide band. You could also use carving tools or even epoxy some glass jewels into holes.

INCLUDE SOME COVES. If you wish, you can further embellish the goblet with a series of shallow coves, cut with a spindle gouge.

MOVE ON TO THE STEM AND FOOT. Shape the rest of the goblet with a spindle gouge. Then make a parting cut at the base, as shown here. For now, part in only to the diameter of the chuck jaws.

COMPLETE THE EMBELLISHMENT. One way to make the goblet look ancient is to char it with a propane torch (top). After some sanding, apply the colors (above). Rubbing away the paint to expose the charred wood makes for an instant antique.

PART OFF. Once the decorations are complete, part off the goblet. Widen the parting cut as you go deeper. This gives you room to slip in sandpaper, as shown. I've wrapped the abrasive around a flexible metal ruler to sand the concave base.

READY FOR POTIONS. Here's the completed goblet. I painted the inside reddish in the depths to imply heat and fire.

7 Embellish the base. Sketch your ideas in pencil and work to those lines. If you don't like the results, sand them off and try something else. I did more carving with the Dremel tool, then charred the surface with a propane torch. Be sure to vacuum up all the shavings and dust before waving around a flame. (There's more about charring wood on p. 178). After a light sanding, I slapped on some gold, blue, and red acrylic paint, rubbing the surface back to reveal some of the charring to give the goblet an ancient and worn look.

8 Sand the bottom and part off. Widen and deepen the parting cut so you can get into the gap with abrasives. To sand inside a narrow space, wrap abrasive around something stiff but bendable, like a steel ruler. Finally, part or saw off the completed goblet and sand away the nub in the center of the base.

BILBOQUET

A bilboquet, or cup and ball, is an ancient catching game. A ball attached to a cup on the end of a stick is swung into the air, then caught and balanced on the cup. A beginner's bilboquet will have a large cup to catch a small ball. For experienced players, a large ball with a small cup presents more of a challenge.

As a teenager, I spent hours improving my hand–eye coordination and reflexes playing with a bilboquet. The cup was small, about ¾ in. (19mm) in diameter; the ball was about 3 in. (75mm) in diameter. The string joining the two was about a foot long. I could soon land the ball on the cup every time. Eventually, with a flick of the wrist, I managed to stab the pointy end of the stick into a hole in the ball, another ancient variation of the game.

You can turn the handle between centers, provided you have a conical tail center that allows you to turn right into the point. If you use a mini spur drive, you'll be able to test the fit of the pointy end into the hole in the ball. The alternative is to mount the blank in a chuck so you can hollow the cup without the tailstock getting in the way.

CHALLENGING GAME. Swinging the large ball so that it lands on the small cup is not as easy as it looks.

CHALLENGE AND
STORAGE. If you
want a greater chal-
lenge, try to land the
hole in the ball on the
narrow end of the
handle. The hole
serves as a place to
put the handle when
not in use.

Turn the Cup and Handle

This part of the bilboquet is a sort of chunky goblet without a base. For kids younger than 10, a typical turned goblet combined with a small ball might be ideal. You need a blank about 10 in. (250mm) long and a conical tail center to support it. The thickness of the blank depends on how big you want the cup. A blank that's ¾ in. (19mm) square will be sufficient for a competitive teenager; for a 7- to 10-year-old, a 2-in. (50mm) square blank might be better.

1 To avoid wasting any of the blank, turn the square to a cylinder between centers, then mount it in a chuck so you can turn the exposed end into a cup.

2 With the cylinder mounted in a chuck, you can still use a conical tail center to center and support it. The slightest catch can dislodge the blank, so keep the tail center in place while you hollow the cup. Use a ⅜-in. (9mm) spindle gouge to cut from the rim into the center. Keep the bevel rubbing and the gouge flute rolled over to about 45 degrees. Roll the tool right on its side as you come into the center and turn the cone free (see the top photo on p. 148).

ROUGH OUT THE CUP. Use a spindle gouge, riding its bevel, to begin shaping the cup. A conical center supports the wood. As you near center, roll the gouge on its side to cut the center waste free, as shown.

If you're extremely nervous about catching the gouge, you can reposition the tail center at the bottom of the cup now. However, it's much better to back off or remove the tailstock so you can use a round-nose scraper to finish shaping the cup (see the left photo below). Use your thumb primarily as a pivot for the tool as it eases the tool forward. Keep your fingers on top of the blank to dampen any vibration arising from using the scraper too forcefully.

Use a skew chisel long point to decorate the inside of the cup with grooves surrounding the conical hole left by the tail center (photo below). The grooves make the cone at center look decorative rather than like a mark left by the tail center. Keep the tool flat on the rest and ease the point into the wood very carefully.

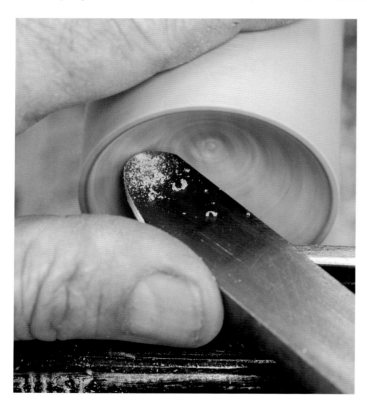

SCRAPE TO FINISH. A round-nose scraper is a good tool for finishing the cup. It leaves a smooth surface and is much less likely to catch than a gouge.

SIMPLE ADORNMENTS. Shallow grooves cut with a skew chisel help make the conical hole left by the tail center appear to be a planned decorative detail.

SHAPE THE OUTSIDE. With the handle mounted between centers, use a skew chisel to shape the outside of the cup. Continue with the skew to add details to the handle.

FINISH THE HANDLE. Use the skew chisel to shape the remainder of the handle. When you're ready to part off, use your thumb to keep the handle from hitting the tool rest, as shown.

3 Mount the blank between centers, with the tail center seated in the bottom of the cup and the spur drive in its original location. Rough out the handle using a gouge or skew chisel. Turn the profile of the cup and the details immediately below. Finish the handle and part it off. Keep your thumb between the handle and the tool rest so the handle doesn't inadvertently hit the rest.

SECURE DRILLING. Use a drill press to drill holes in the ball for the cord. Steady the ball by resting it on a piece of scrap that has a round hole in it. Here, I'm drilling a hole for the handle. In the center of that will be a smaller hole for the cord. Drill into endgrain.

Tether the Ball to the Cup

You can learn how to turn a sphere on pp. 98–105. Once you have it shaped and sanded, you have to drill some holes.

You have to make a two-step hole, the larger part being for the knot in the cord. And, on larger balls, you have to drill a hole partway through for the handle. The ball can be drilled on the lathe, using a drill held in a drill chuck in the tailstock and the ball in a jam chuck. That's risky, though, because the ball can easily come loose in the chuck. It's much safer to use a drill press, with the ball located in a circular hole to steady it. Drill into the endgrain to ensure a clean exit hole.

On small balls without a hole for the handle, the larger portion of the hole should be just wide enough to accommodate the knot that prevents the cord from being pulled through the smaller hole. Pass the end of the cord through the small hole first, put a knot in the end, and pull the knot back into the ball.

On larger balls, drill the hole for the handle first, then drill the smaller hole for the cord in the center of the first hole. Again, put the cord through the smaller hole first, then pull the knot back into the hole for the handle.

HIDE THE KNOT. Drill a narrow hole through the ball for the cord. At one end, drill a shallow larger hole, making a recess to hold the knot in the cord.

A CUP AND BALL FOR BEGINNERS. A ball that fits inside a cup is best for younger kids new to the game.

SPINNING TOPS

The simple endgrain spinning top is one of the best projects for developing your turning techniques. Tops may look simple but they are definitely not as easy as they look, especially if you want a decent finish off the tool and a nice sharp point on which the top can spin. It's not a project for scrapers or scraping techniques: Spinning tops demand slicing cuts. If you push the tool into the cut, especially near center, you'll either tear the endgrain, have a catch that pulls the piece off the lathe, or, if you're lucky, induce chatter marks severe enough to keep as decoration.

SIMPLE SPINNERS. Small tops are irresistible, and spinning them soon becomes competitive, even when you're alone. Turning tops is an excellent way to improve your turning ability.

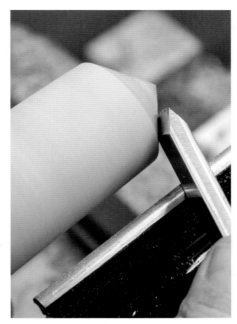

SHAPING WITH A SKEW CHISEL. To shape the cone for the top, use the long point. Be sure to keep the bevel rubbing the wood. To avoid tearing the endgrain at the point of the cone, slow the cut as you approach center.

Spinning tops can be made entirely with a spindle gouge. However, a skew chisel is much handier when it comes to completing the shank and does a better job of turning a sharp point. Above all, you need a lightness of touch when cutting. If you're inclined to go hard at the wood instead of letting the wood come to the tool, turning a few dozen tops will slow you down and make you a better turner.

The ideal diameter for a hand-spun top is between 1⅜ in. and 2 in. (35mm to 50mm). A top can be any shape you like, provided it has a point to spin on and a shank by which to get it spinning. These tops are launched with a snap of the fingers, which is something small children cannot do. Consequently, the younger the child, the fatter the shank needs to be. A shank that's ³⁄₁₆ in. (5mm) in diameter is about right for a 6-year-old; competitive teenagers who can snap their fingers go for a ¹⁄₁₆-in. (2mm) shank, which launches the top with some real momentum.

Don't make the shank too fancy; it is rolled between your fingers, so sharp detail makes that painful. A bulbous end to the shank may look attractive, but it doesn't make spinning the top any easier.

Turn a Top

Select a blank no more than 2 in. (50mm) square projecting about 4 in. (100mm) from the chuck; that's enough wood for two tops. If the blank is any longer, it's too easy to have a catch that launches it into space. As always, true the blank. Whenever you have even the slightest catch, you need to true the blank again before continuing.

1 Begin by turning a cone on the endgrain, using either a skew chisel or a ⅜-in. (9mm) spindle gouge.

If you use a skew chisel (see the photos above), pivot the long point into the wood to start the cut and continue using the point to

SHAPING WITH A GOUGE—1. Begin with the tool on its side, then roll it counter-clockwise to take a heavier cut, as shown.

SHAPING WITH A GOUGE—2. Create details with the nose of the gouge on its side, as shown (top). Bring the tool in from the right to shape the other side of the groove. Finish by making the sharp point at the end of the cone (above).

about halfway to center. Be sure to keep the bevel on the wood. As you approach center, raise the tool handle so you cut with the edge. If you push the edge into the cut faster than the wood is coming to the tool, you'll feel little tugs; that's endgrain being pulled out. Ease the tool forward ever more slowly until you stop at center, when no more wood comes to the edge. If you push the edge across center and tweak out the fibers, you won't get a sharp point on the cone and the top won't spin true or for very long.

If you use a gouge, you can create an ogee, or an S-shaped curve. Start the tool on its side as you pivot the nose into the wood. As you go down the slope, rotate the gouge slightly counterclockwise for a heavier cut, bringing it back on its side to create a groove. To cut the right-hand side of the groove, roll the gouge over and pivot the point in from the right. Finally, roll the gouge over again to refine the sharp point.

2 Turn the top of the cone. You can use a skew chisel, but a gouge is less likely to catch as you hog out the waste. Make space by cutting in from either side. Take care not to get the shank supporting the cone too thin too soon; otherwise, a clean cut on the top of the cone is near impossible, because the heavy end will wobble no matter how light your touch.

The shank needs to be at least ¼ in. (6mm) in diameter when you make the final cut to shape the top of the cone. You get only one go at this. Start the gouge on its side, lining the bevel up in the direction you want to cut (see the top photo on p. 156). Pivot the edge in to the wood, then rotate the gouge slightly clockwise for a heavier cut. End the cut with the gouge right on its side, so you don't catch the left wing. The gouge nose reduces the shank diameter to about ⅛ in. (3mm). If you try to make the cut again, chatter marks are inevitable because the cone has almost no support. If you failed to true the rim, there is little you can do about it now, and you'll need to start over.

TOP THE CONE. Use a gouge to begin shaping the top of the cone and make space for the final cut, working from either side. Just don't go too deep at this point.

FINAL CUTS. Be sure the rim of the cone is true—you won't be able to fix it later. To finish the top of the cone, begin with a gouge on its side (above left). Roll the tool for a heavier cut (above right), and finish with the tool on its side again, leaving about ⅛ in. (3mm) of wood for the shank (right).

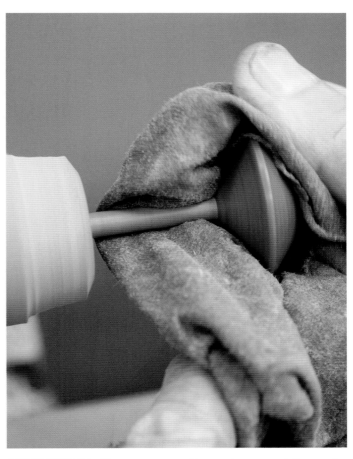

SPINDLE OPTIONS. You can use a gouge for the shank, but a skew chisel (shown) will leave a smoother finish. Support the thin turning with your fingers.

APPLY POLISH. Always use your fingers to support the work when sanding or applying the finish. Here, I'm applying my favorite mixture of beeswax and boiled linseed oil.

3 Turn the shank. You can complete the shank using a ³⁄₈-in. (9mm) spindle gouge, but you will achieve a much better finish if you use a ¹⁄₂-in. (13mm) skew chisel. Whichever one you choose, you must support the slender stem with your forefinger.

4 Sand and polish. With a comparatively heavy cone on the slender shaft, any force against the lathe axis is likely to heave the top free. So, when sanding and polishing, balance any pressure against the wood with equal pressure on the other side of the shaft or cone. When parting off the completed top, have your fingers around the top to catch it as it's cut free (see the top photo on p. 158). A careful parting cut should leave you with a point on the end. If not, sand the end round so you can spin the top either way up.

PART TO A POINT.
Use a skew chisel to part off the top, aiming to make a point on the end.

TWO-WAY TWIRLERS.
With a rounded or pointed end to the spindle, you can spin the tops right-side up or upside-down. It's the same flick of the fingers with your palm up instead of down.

BALANCE TRAY

The balance tray is a variation on a classic puzzle that helps us develop hand–eye coordination. The tray has a grid of nine shallow holes and contains nine loose marbles. The aim is to tilt the tray this way and that to roll the marbles into all the holes.

The tray needs a rim to contain the marbles, and on the rim of the base there is a cove that makes the tray easy to lift. To make the game more difficult, the center hole on this board is at the top of a barely discernible rise, making it quite difficult to seat the larger marble. (So it's not a disaster if you can't turn a flat surface; you

SIMPLE YET CHALLENGING. Rolling all nine marbles into their holes is not as easy as it looks—especially with larger marbles. Made from ash, the tray is 7⅜ in. (190mm) in diameter and 1 in. (25mm) high. The marbles sit in ½-in. (13mm) holes.

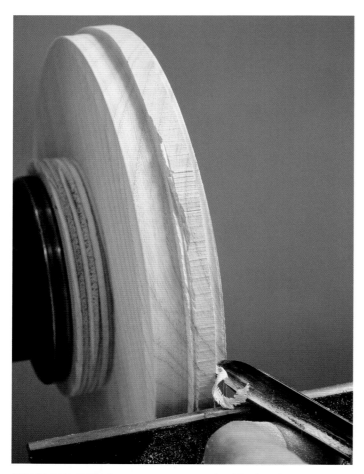

SHALLOW ATTACHMENT. Because the blank is fairly thin, the screws holding it can't penetrate very deeply. Here, I've used plywood disks with a screw chuck so that the screw goes into the blank only ¼ in. (6mm). I'm using a gouge to true the rim.

WASTE LINE. A pencil line on the rim, started at the thinnest point, shows you how much wood to remove to true the face.

simply get a more challenging game.) This board also has a slight slope from the four corner holes to the rim. When the tray is flat, all the marbles roll to the rim.

A balance tray is a facework project. You need a blank about 8 in. (200mm) in diameter and 1 in. to 1½ in. (25mm to 38mm) thick, with the grain running across the face. Mount the blank on a screw chuck or faceplate with the screw or screws penetrating the wood as little as possible. If you use a screw chuck, flatten the face of the blank so it doesn't rock on the screw.

If you use a faceplate and screws, locate two screws on opposite sides of any ridge to keep the blank from rocking.

1 True the blank and make the base slightly concave. Begin with the rim, cutting in from either face to keep the endgrain from splintering.

Next, true the base. If you are uncertain how much to take off, hold a pencil to the thinnest point and rotate the blank by hand to ensure it is the lowest point. If you have a lot to remove,

TWO CUTS. Using a gouge, make a series of little pull cuts from the rim (top), nibbling toward center to remove most of the waste. Then roll the tool over for a shear cut from the rim to center (above).

A FINAL SCRAPE. Take light cuts with a skewed scraper to make the base slightly concave. This allows the tray to sit flat on the rim.

use a gouge on its side to clear the waste. Then roll the tool over so the bevel rubs on the trued surface for a shear cut into center.

The base needs to be slightly concave so the tray rests on its rim, so take another shear cut with a gouge to achieve that. To finish, I prefer to use a skewed scraper for a very light stroking cut across the face. Be sure the scraper is tilted down so the angle between the top of the blade and the face is less than 90 degrees.

2 Turn a recess for the chuck. Lay out the diameter using dividers and turn a recess no more than ⅛ in. (3mm) deep, using a skew

CREATE A RECESS.
Use dividers to mark
the width of a shallow
recess for chuck jaws.
Then cut the recess
with a skew chisel
held flat on the
tool rest.

**FLATTEN THE
RECESS.** Use a short
straightedge to check
for flatness. A shad-
ow under the edge,
as here, means that
the surface needs
more work.

chisel flat on the rest as a scraper. The long
point of the skew will dovetail the recess to
match the chuck jaws (photo above).

The bottom of the recess needs to be flat for
two reasons. First, so the chuck jaws slot into the
corner between the side and base of the recess;
second, so there is no space behind the jaws.
Space behind the jaws is wasted because it
reduces the depth to which you can hollow the
inside when you reverse the blank. You can
check the flatness of the recess with a homemade straightedge (photo at left).

If you have wider chuck jaws, like those
shown on p. 168, you can turn a small bead of a
foot on the base and grip it with the jaws. That
way, you don't have to hollow into the base at
all, giving you much more margin for error
when drilling holes for the marbles.

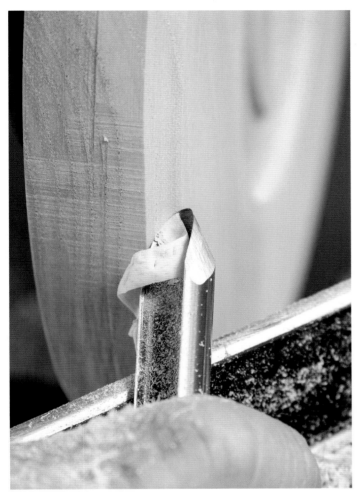

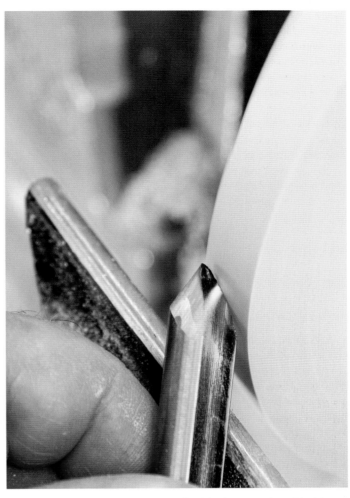

SHAPE A COVE. Take a series of shear cuts with a gouge to form a cove on the rim. This will make it easy to pick up the tray.

REVERSE AND RE-TRUE. Turn the blank around and hold it with the chuck jaws. Then use a gouge to skim and true the rim. Keep the tool on its side for a shear scrape. If you try this with the flute up, you're guaranteed to have a monumental catch.

3 Use a gouge to turn a cove on the rim of the base. Hold the gouge on the tool rest and swing the edge in an arc through the wood for a shear cut.

4 Sand and finish the base.

5 Reverse the piece, holding it by expanding the chuck jaws in the recess. True the rim again. A re-chucked piece usually runs slightly out of whack, so it needs skimming. You can shear scrape with a scraper or a ½-in. (13mm) spindle gouge rolled on its side.

RECESS THE FACE.
To cut away the middle of the face, use a square-end scraper with a slightly radiused edge. Keep one corner clear of the surface you're cutting. Ease the edge straight into the wood and you should achieve the typical shaving and finish shown here.

LAY OUT A GRID. On the lathe, mark equally spaced circles on the face. Then, off the lathe, draw two straight lines—one with the grain, one at 90 degrees to the first (as shown here). I find I can work more accurately if I have a tiny circle to define center, rather than a dot. I also like to shade the area near the rim where I don't want any holes. You can subdivide the quadrants to locate other centers.

6 Use a square-end scraper to turn a flat surface surrounded by a rim about ¼ in. (6mm) wide and high enough to contain the marbles you have. I prefer to use a ¾-in. (19mm) square-end scraper to turn a flat surface (see the top photo above). Inevitably, the surface will have some undulations at first. If you hold a straightedge against the spinning surface, you'll burnish the high spots, showing you what needs to be removed to make the surface flat. If you

leave the surface smooth but undulating, you make the task of rolling marbles into the holes a lot trickier.

7 Lay out positions for the holes. On the lathe, mark several equally spaced circles and center. Off the lathe, draw one line through center aligned with the grain, and another at right angles, also through center.

I could use compasses to locate the second line precisely, but I find it just as easy to use the lines etched on the ruler. I can always check distances between the points where the straight lines intersect with the outer circle. My aim is to lay out a grid based on center, then decide which intersections will be the centers for the marble holes. No rule dictates the number or position of the holes, but fewer might be better than too many.

8 Drill the holes at the drill press so you can set the depth and keep them vertical. A sawtooth bit with a spur cuts a very clean hole. I don't worry about the mark left by the spur, but you could easily cover it with a leather disk or round self-adhesive label. The ½-in. (13mm) holes shown in the top photo at right are for marbles that range from ⅝ in. to 1³⁄₁₆ in. (16mm to 30mm). The holes need to be just deep enough to keep the marbles from hitting the bottom.

9 Put the tray back on the chuck and sand it. Because of the holes, the surface needs an oil finish. If you put a block of wax to the spinning surface, wax collects in the holes and is difficult to clear up. This tray is oiled with boiled linseed oil.

DRILL. Use a drill press to keep the holes vertical and uniformly deep.

THE FINISHED BALANCE TRAY. Larger marbles and smaller holes make the game more difficult. With this set, the large marble in the center needs to be in position before the last pair of the inner four.

TABLE SKITTLES

The game of skittles has been around for thousands of years, spawning innumerable variations. In every version of the game, the aim is to knock over a group of pins, usually five or nine in number, set on a grid. In most variations of skittles, you roll a ball at the pins, but you can also throw small barrels or cylinders if there is no smooth ground. And then there's the swinger's version common in British pubs.

The variation known as table skittles, or Devil Amongst the Tailors, is centuries old and derived from the even older game of alley skittles. In table skittles, a ball or knocker is swung clockwise around a pole, aiming to knock over the nine pins as the knocker returns to the player, who catches it in readiness for another go. Players get three swings of the ball in each turn, scoring points based on how many pins they knock over. The maximum score in one go is 27. The pins are reset at the beginning of a turn or when all nine have been knocked over. As ever, if you want rules and ways of scoring, you can find many variations on the Internet.

Everything in this table version is turned. It has a heavy base so the pins stay upright as the knocker swings around the pole. On the flat central platform, inlaid dowels define the grid for the pins. Because the knocker travels in an arc around the post, the cap has to be able to rotate freely atop the post. A moat around the central platform stores the pins and catches them as they fall. On large boards, you can turn a wider and more effective pin-catcher moat.

TABLE SKITTLES. Although only 14 in. (355mm) in diameter, this compact set of table skittles works well. The post is 28 in. (710mm) tall.

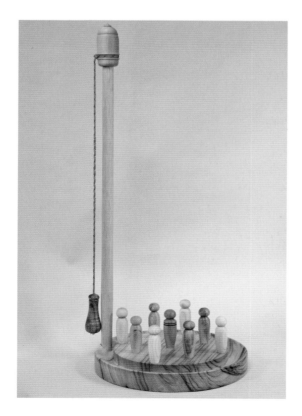

Turn the Base

You need a blank at least 14 in. (355mm) in diameter and 2 in. (50mm) thick. Choose a wood known for stability, like the camphor laurel shown in the photos. Well-seasoned oak, ash, cherry, or walnut are other good options. If the base warps, the pins won't stand up. If you have the lathe for it, scale this up closer to 24 in. (610mm) in diameter, possibly laminating the blanks to ensure stability. A larger diameter allows you to have a wider moat around the pin platform. Of course, a larger base means you need a taller post and more space needed to swing the knocker.

1 Mount the blank on a faceplate or hold it on a screw chuck. Your main concern is to limit the number of screw holes penetrating what will be the flat platform for the pins. A single hole at center can be plugged later, but the screws in a faceplate might not be on the same circumference or match the grid you want for your pins. For no screw hole in the final base, use the outer holes on a large faceplate (which few of us have), or a disk of MDF attached to a faceplate. True the MDF rim and mark a circle on which to locate the screws; then you lose the screw holes when you turn the moat around the central platform.

Once you have your blank on the lathe, use a gouge to true the rim (top photo at right). Next, turn the bottom slightly concave so the base will rest on its rim. Then turn a recess in which to expand a chuck. The larger the diameter you can grip, the more secure the fixing and the shallower the recess can be. As always, check that the bottom of the recess is flat so the chuck jaws seat right in the corner of the dovetail. Note that for jaws with a crisp dovetail on the rim, the recess need not be more than 1/8 in. (3mm) deep, especially when the jaws support more than half the diameter of the blank.

With the base completed, sand and finish the bottom.

TRUE THE RIM. Work in from either face to prevent tearout at the corners.

MAKE A RECESS. With the base turned slightly concave, mark a recess for the largest chuck jaws you have. Here, I'm measuring for a set of 8¼-in. (210mm) jaws. Use a short straightedge to be sure the bottom of the recess is flat.

GET A DECENT GRIP. Large jaws grip a wide diameter, preventing the blank from flexing as you flatten the face.

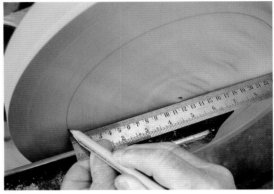

BEGIN PIN LAYOUT. Mark a circle to show the outermost pins. Be sure to leave sufficient room on the rim for the post.

LAY OUT THE GRID. Draw a line through center and another at right angles to it, intersecting the circle. Use dividers to check the intersections are equally spaced, as shown. Connect the intersections and locate centers for all the pins.

2 Remount the blank on the expanding jaws and flatten the top face.

3 Lay out the grid for the pins. Begin by marking a circle to locate the outermost pins on the grid. Be sure you have space enough on the rim for the post. A 14-in. (355mm) board is a trifle cramped, but with a minimal moat I can put a grid $6^{11}/_{16}$ in. (170mm) square on a platform $10^{1}/_{4}$ in. (260mm) in diameter.

With the board off the lathe, finish the grid for the pins. Draw a line through the center, then another at right angles to it. Check the accuracy of your drawing with dividers, measuring the distance between the points where the lines intersect the circle. When you are satisfied that the intersections are evenly spaced around the circle, draw a square to connect those points, then pinpoint the center of each side.

4 At the drill press, drill shallow holes for the inlaid dowels and the post. Use a sawtooth bit for a clean and accurate hole. For the dowel holes, I used a $^{1}/_{4}$-in. (6mm) drill because it fits the hole left by the screw chuck. For the post, drill a larger hole in line with one of the diagonals. I use a $1^{1}/_{4}$-in. (32mm) bit for that hole.

5 Glue dowels into the holes. You can use ready-made dowels or, if you possess dowel cutters, make your own. Make cross-grain dowels so the grain is aligned with the blank.

GLUE IN THE DOWELS. These pin markers can be ready-made or you can make your own. You need a wood for the dowels that contrasts with the base.

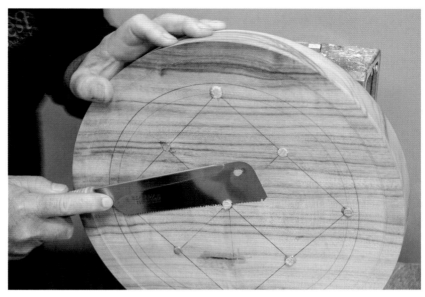

MARK AND TRIM. Draw a circle to define the inner edge of the moat. Then, with the lathe off, trim the dowels flush with the base, as shown.

6 Complete the turning. Mount the base on the chuck again and define the inner edge of the moat by drawing a circle just clear of the inlaid dowels. With the lathe off, trim the dowels nearly flush with the platform.

Use a spindle or bowl gouge to rough out the moat and define the platform. On a wider board, the moat can be rounded or even square if the rim is wide enough for the post hole. Level the platform using a skewed scraper. Check for flatness by holding a steel straightedge to the spinning wood, as shown in the bottom photo at right. The edge will burnish any high spots, which you can quickly eliminate with a few gentle passes with a scraper.

When the platform is level, clean up the moat using a gouge and a few delicate shear cuts.

GOUGE AND FLATTEN. Use a gouge to shape the moat (left). Then flatten the face of the base with a skewed scraper. Hold a straightedge against the spinning wood to reveal any high spots (bottom), seen here as pale streaks above the ruler, opposite 60 and 70.

CLEAN THE MOAT. Finish turning the moat by taking shear cuts with a gouge, cutting in from each rim toward the bottom.

7 Sand and finish the base. To maintain the flat surface, use a rigid sanding block to back the abrasive. A slight mound usually develops at center, so stop the lathe and push the blocked abrasive across center, rotating the base by hand a few degrees each time.

Turn the Cap

Select a blank about 1 in. (25mm) larger in diameter than the post and 4 in. (100mm) long.

There is a chicken and egg situation with the post and cap as to which comes first. The cap has to rotate freely on top of the post, so the inside needs to be cylindrical. It's more accurate to drill the inside, rather than turn it, so that's what I do. You'll also get a much better fit by refining the top of the post to fit into the cap, rather than finding a drill only fractionally larger than the post. For jobs like this, I turn the outside first, incorporating a detail that matches the chuck diameter. Then I remount the piece with the chuck jaws clamped on the detail so I can drill out the inside. That way everything is concentric and I take a finished piece from the chuck with no need for handwork off the lathe.

1 Use calipers to establish a diameter that matches the internal diameter of your chuck jaws. When you reverse the cap in the chuck, this is the diameter the jaws will grip. The jaws won't mark the wood if the diameter on the cap is the diameter of the chuck or fractionally smaller. Any larger, and there will be teeth marks from the jaw corners. Shape the outside of the cap up to the chuck jaws, maintaining the measured diameter to the right of where a decorative bead will go. Sand and finish what you can of the outside before reversing the cap in the chuck.

BEGIN THE CAP. Turn a cylinder, then turn a tenon at one end, sized to the inside diameter of chuck jaws. Use calipers to check the size.

SHAPE THE TOP. As you turn the top of the cap, be sure to maintain a portion of the tenon diameter to fit the chuck. Here, the top curves in to the small bead, so the chuck jaws can sit in a shallow groove as they butt against the bead.

2 With the cap reversed in the chuck, drill into the endgrain at least 2 in. (50mm), using a Forstner or sawtooth bit. Then sand and polish the hole using a sanding stick. You could break your finger if you wrap it in abrasive and stick it in a small hole with the lathe running. The sanding stick is a dowel rod with a slit up the center cut on a bandsaw. Slide one end of the abrasive into the slot and wrap the rest around the stick. Use the same stick to poke the polishing rag into the hole.

3 Complete the outside. The cap needs a groove for the cord, so use a ⅜-in. (9mm) spindle gouge to turn a cove, cutting in from either side with the flute facing the center of the cove. Be sure to start the gouge on its side. To create a bead on each side of the cove, use the long point of a skew chisel to cut a small groove, then take planing cuts to remove the waste to the bottom of the groove. Use abrasives to round over the bead as you finish the cap.

Turn the Post

Post blanks need to be 1⅜ in. to 1½ in. (35mm to 40mm) square. The length depends on what you can fit on your lathe and the diameter of your base.

For this size of table skittles, the post needs to be at least 28 in. (710mm) long so the swinging knocker can reach every pin. The taller the post, the longer the cord with the knocker needs to be and, consequently, the flatter the arc of the swing. A short cord means that the knocker swings through a tighter arc and may not reach all the pins. The drawing on p. 172 will help you determine the height of both the post and pins for the diameter of the board you are turning.

Such a long spindle is not easy to turn, so it's not surprising that a length of dowel or broom handle often serves as the post. It's a simple but clunky solution; a shaped post is far more elegant. The only requirement is that the bottom end fit snugly into the hole in the base: tight but not so tight that it's hard to push in.

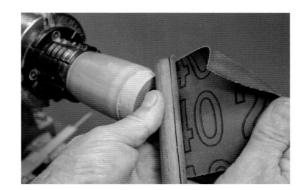

SAND SAFELY. Wrap abrasive around a sanding stick and use it to smooth the inside of the hole. That's much safer than poking your finger into the small hole.

CUT A COVE. Working from either side with a gouge, create a cove that will hold the cord for the knocker.

SWING AWAY. The knocker in full swing, busting through the pins.

POST SIZES

Once you know where the grid sits in relation to the post, you can calculate the height of the post to ensure that the knocker reaches every pin.

Post

48 in.

Cap heights

36 in.

28 in.

28 in.

36 in.

48 in.

6 in.
Pin height
4 in.

20 in.   16 in.   12 in.   8 in.   4 in.   0 in.

Distance from post

FREE SPINS. A domed or conical end on the post reduces friction so the cap spins freely.

The top of the post needs to be a cylinder very slightly smaller than the cap fitting over it. Making the end conical or domed reduces friction. You want the cap free to spin on the post, but not rattling loose, and this is much easier to achieve fitting the post to the cap, rather than the cap to the post. The bottom of the post can be as fancy as you like. I favor long elegant curves, but if you prefer a pile of beads or some variant of a baluster, go for it.

This set of skittles has the longest post I can put between centers on my lathe. The ends were turned to size using a 1-in. (25mm) skew chisel, first peeling, then shear-cutting for the final cuts and a smooth surface (see the top photo on p. 174). For the rest of the turning, you'll need to use grips that equalize any tool pressure against the wood, as for the croquet mallet handle and thin dowel on pp. 33, 39, 118, or you might resort to a 3-point steady rest like the one shown on p. 119.

A LONG POLE IN SECTIONS

If you need a post longer than your lathe can handle, join two lengths using a short piece of brass or copper plumbing tube. Turn the ends of the post sections to be joined so the tube fits on tight. Then fit the tube over one section and mount the assembly on the lathe so you can turn the rest of the post to match the tube's diameter. Repeat for the other section. The tube goes over a conical drive.

You can true the ends of copper, brass, or aluminium tube on the lathe, using tools made of high-speed steel. Hold a short length of tube in pin jaws, with the lathe running about 1,200 rpm. Keep a skew chisel flat on the rest and use either the long point or the bevel side to true each end and chamfer the inner lip.

METAL CONNECTOR. A short piece of copper tubing makes a good connector for the skittles post. The post sections are epoxied into the metal.

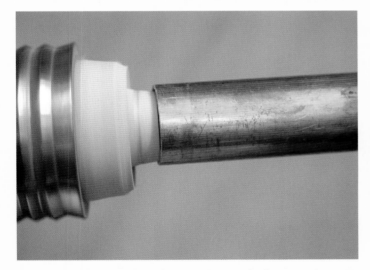

FINAL FITTING. Fit the tube over one end of a post, then mount the assembly on the lathe. The free end of the tube fits over a conical drive center. Turn the post down to match the inside diameter of the tube.

TRUING SOFT METALS. You can shape soft metals with tools made of high-speed steel, like this skew. Use either the long point or the bevel side to chamfer the end of the tube.

ENDS FIRST. Use a skew chisel to size the ends of the post, then shape the remainder. Use a sizing gauge, as shown, for accuracy.

Turn the Knocker

A traditional knocker is a ball on the end of a chain, but there is no reason why it can't be more like a blind or light pull, fastened to a cord. Consequently, I offer you a more oblong knocker that adds heft to a lightweight cord.

You need a squared blank about 1½ in. (40mm) in diameter and 3½ in. (90mm) long. Stand the blank on end and drill a hole through the center that is wide enough for the cord. Then enlarge one end to accommodate and hide the knotted end of the cord. Alternatively, you

can put the blank in a chuck and drill on the lathe, starting with the larger hole. Either way, once you've drilled the holes, mount the blank between conical centers, so you know the holes are dead center, and turn it to a shape you like.

Turn the Pins

Pin blanks need to be at least 1³⁄₁₆ in. by 4 in. (30mm by 100mm) with straight grain running the length of the blank.

Small pins are fairly basic spindle work that you can make with a ¾-in. (19mm) skew chisel and a thin parting tool. Reduce the blank to a sized cylinder and then use dividers to mark out the length. Use a parting tool to cut straight in at each end to define the length.

To save grabbing a ruler and pencil, I position the groove/neck a tool-width away from the end. It's a simple measuring trick you can often use when laying out beads and grooves on spindles. When you're making a set of pins, keep the first one handy so you can check progress as you match one to the other. I used the diameter of the spur drive to gauge the foot of these pins. Be sure to retain the left side of the parting cut, so when it comes to parting off you can continue the original cut.

TURN THE KNOCKER. Drill for the cord, then use those holes to hold the blank between conical centers to do the shaping.

SIMPLE MEASURE. Use the width of a tool, like the skew shown here, to gauge the size of the pin's head.

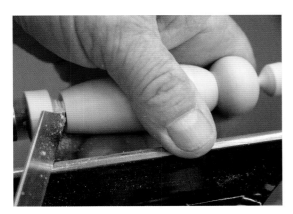

PART OFF THE PIN. Make this cut at an angle, to be sure the pin sits flat on its base.

Sand and polish the pin, then part off at an angle to ensure the pin has a concave base. Hold your thumb on the rest to keep the pin clear as it comes free. To finish the other end, you'll need to saw off the waste and hand-sand.

Assembling Table Skittles

The post can be glued or jammed in position, depending on whether you want the set to be transportable. When setting up the knocker on its cord, first get the knocker pulled over the knot that keeps it on the cord, then tie the other end to the cap. The knocker should rest just clear of the platform on which the pegs stand. Put the peg farthest from the post on its spot and make sure it's within range of the knocker.

Other Skittle Games

When you have reasonably smooth ground or a hard floor, you can roll balls at the pins. Played indoors, a simple backstop to catch both pins and balls can prevent damage to furniture and baseboards and make it easier to retrieve both balls and pins.

In France, an eight-pin variation is played with mallets, making it a cross between croquet and ground billiards. There's a good chance that anyone with a collection of balls, pins, mallets, and hoops will develop his or her own game,

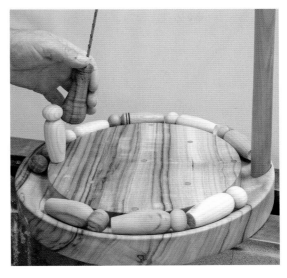

CHECK THE SWING. On any skittles set, the knocker should rest just above the base. At the end of its swing, it should connect with the outermost pin.

possibly with golfing overtones if you include a few holes.

A traditional variation of skittles is to knock the pins over with small elongated barrels, known as "pigs," seen to the right in the photo below. These can be rolled or thrown underarm. Or you can toss "sticks," which are the short cylinders to the left. In a game of 5-pins, pins are valued by the number of grooves.

OTHER KINDS OF KNOCKERS. Two of the many variations of skittles use barrel-shaped "pigs" (right foreground) or "sticks" (left foreground) thrown or rolled at the pins to knock them over.

FINAL TOUCHES

This final chapter offers a few thoughts on finishing and the embellishing techniques that involve burning, carving, painting, and drawing.

Finishing

I am not an authority on finishes, but there are many books on the topic and heaps of advice on the Internet. I've tried quite a few finishes, but I realized early on in my turning career that I don't like hard finishes involving carnauba wax or sealers that deteriorate after a few years. I mainly use variations on the wax finish I was shown on my first day at the lathe, back in January 1970.

WAX AND OIL

At first, I used a paraffin-wax candle on the spinning wood, but soon opted for beeswax because it smells nicer. It also sounds more user-friendly on the care label I stick to the bottom of most of my bowls. Beeswax is a soft finish that benefits from ongoing attention and a bit of wax polish whenever the wood looks dull. Weekly application of almost any wax polish for a few months will give the wood a glowing patina that you cannot get out of a bottle or can; after that, polishing every couple of months will be sufficient.

With work that can be finished on the lathe, I slop on oil (most often linseed) to fill the grain, usually with the lathe off or running slowly so the oil doesn't spray too far. Then I wipe off the excess and apply a lump of beeswax to the spinning wood. This creates a sticky layer that mixes with the oil when I friction-melt it into the wood with a rag. If the wood has holes, either natural or drilled, I omit the wax and simply buff the wood with a cloth. Wax collects in the holes and is difficult or tedious to remove. Dense, close-grained woods don't need oil, so it's sufficient to apply wax or simply rub with a very waxy rag.

FOOD-SAFE FINISHES

As a bowl turner, I have always been concerned about toxins in finishes. For years I used either vegetable cooking oil or mineral oil. I have used walnut and macadamia oil, but these days we know that many people are allergic to nuts, so I tend to avoid nut oils. Some children are allergic to dairy-based products like milk paint, which contains casein.

Mineral oil is a laxative, although not in the amounts you might lick off a bowl, but it sounds a bit industrial, so I rarely use it. For at least twenty years I've used boiled linseed oil as a base on just about everything, having ascertained that it's not known to be carcinogenic or

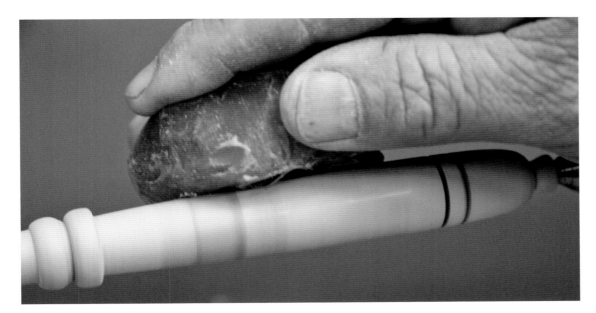

A SIMPLE TWO-STEP FINISH. After flooding the piece with oil, hold beeswax against the spinning wood (left), then a rag (below). The friction will melt the oil–wax mixture into the wood.

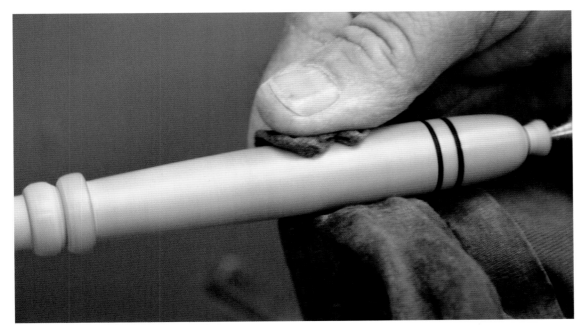

toxic once dry. Rags soaked in boiled linseed oil can combust spontaneously. I've never had a problem, but I do keep my polishing rags clear of piles of shavings and spread out so they can dry. They are too stiff to use in a couple of days. Bundled up, oily rags can build up enough heat to smolder, then burst into flame.

A number of commercially available finishes are marketed as food safe. Many are somewhat dangerous to apply because they emit noxious fumes or contain volatile compounds, but virtually all are non-toxic when cured. Lead and mercury are rarely in modern finishes; still, check the list of contents on any product you purchase.

Burning

Charring wood can add character and change your perception of an object. There are several ways to apply enough heat to your turnings to char the surface.

WOOD BURNING. You can hold piano wire against the wood to char a line. Or you can press the thin edge of a hardwood wedge into a groove, as shown here.

FRICTION

Friction can blacken grooves in a few seconds. Black lines can add style to a spindle or smarten a wheel hub. Specialty woodturning stores offer piano wire with a couple of knobs to grab as you pull the wire against a spindle. I prefer to use a thin slice of hardwood, pressing it into the groove, as shown at left. The friction should quickly generate enough heat to char the wood. There will be lots of smoke. The charring fuzzes the edges of the groove, so sand after the charring for sharp, well-defined rims. On an end-grain face like a wheel hub, use a thin stick like a very long match. Expect up to an inch to wear away as you build up heat.

TORCHING

More exciting is using a propane torch to burn the surface. If you want to do this with the work on the lathe as I do, it is essential that you vacuum the area clear of shavings before you start and turn off any dust extraction. You don't want a spark to get in the shavings, especially with a jet of air fanning any flame. Much safer is to unscrew the chuck and take the work away from shavings to a concrete floor or metal bench.

Once you have charred the surface, let it cool before turning on the dust extraction and brushing or sanding away the charcoal on the surface. If you want a textured surface, a drill-mounted nylon or wire brush rotating against the wood spinning on the lathe is very effective, as is heavy sanding, which removes softer wood, leaving the harder grain in relief. Be warned, this is a really messy business. Even with good dust extraction, you can end up looking like an old-time coal miner coming off a shift.

When the charcoal is removed and no black transfers to your hand when you rub the wood, you can apply the finish of your choice.

Carving

A bit of carving can add some whimsy or style to your turned forms. My carving tends to be very fast, loose, and basic, done to transform the smooth and modern into the battered and antique. On the goblet cup shown here, I used a small carving gouge to cut grooves running with the grain. For grooves across the grain and running around the cup, I prefer to use a Dremel tool with a cylindrical burr; it gives me greater control. The photos at right show how to use the tool freehand. You could mount the Dremel in a jig for a more consistent line, but the carving would lose its spontaneity.

The Dremel is also pivoted in to cut the flat top and rounded slots around the base of the same cup. Again, you could set the Dremel in a pivoting jig for a very precise cut, but here I don't want that, and anyway the marks will be further distorted by burning.

SMALL GRIND. A Dremel tool lets you add embellishments quickly. I position the tool on the rest and pivot it into the work to break up a bead (left), or add a series of slots (below). Hold the work in position and rotate it by hand.

FINISH WITH FLAME. Heat from a propane torch will quickly char the wood surface. But before you fire up the torch, sweep up all dust and shavings from around the lathe.

SHARP EDGES. For well-defined bands of color, cut shallow grooves in the wood and brush paint between the grooves (right). Let the paint dry, then re-cut the grooves to define the edges (below).

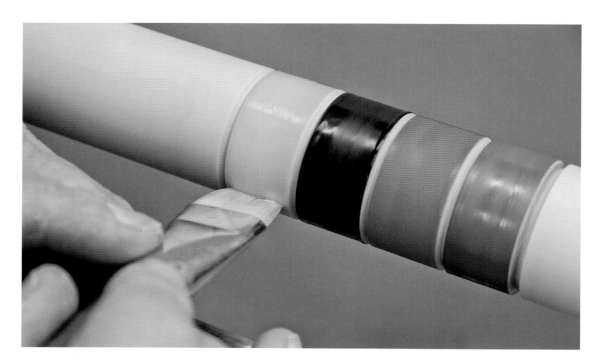

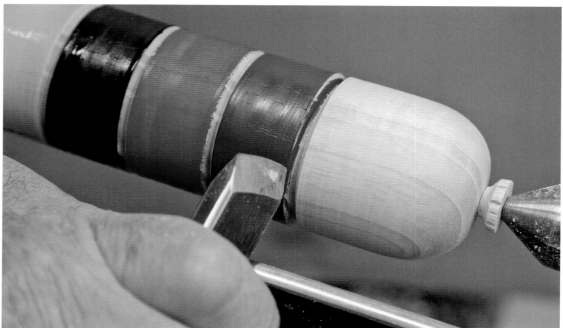

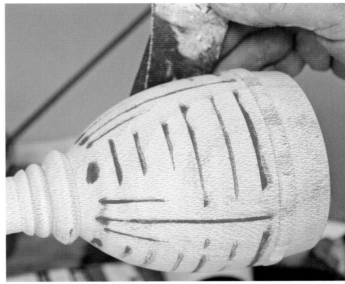

PAINT WITH ABANDON. To add color to grooves, apply paint liberally (above left). Then sand the piece so that paint remains only in the grooves (above right). After I applied the red, I lightly charred the goblet, holding the flame at a tangent to keep it away from the paint. Then I sanded again and added the dollops of thick gold acrylic (left).

Coloring

Color brightens up less exciting woods while adding an extra educational element for toddlers who are learning their colors. Wood can be stained, painted, or dyed, and there are superb books written by people who have used all three techniques over a number of years and can offer much better advice than I can. However, here are a few tips.

You can apply color on the lathe when you want an accurate ring, running the lathe at about 100 rpm. Although the grooves define the bounds of each color, the edges are rarely as well defined as I like. The trick to having a well-defined edge is to re-turn the grooves.

When you want color in a groove, paint inside the grooves with abandon, then sand or turn the form to leave paint only where you want it.

TRANSFORMATION. I sent two rather plain cars (left) plus some plain peggies to my friend Terry Baker for completion. The pine-bodied car came back painted orange, with exhaust pipes and a new and better-equipped driver. The other car was turned over, outfitted with a cowl and rear hump, and painted yellow. The smallish driver is epoxied in place to avoid a choking hazard. Terry carved the grills with a Dremel tool.

Marker pens are handy for making lines, and if you run the lathe slow and move the pen across the surface, you can create spirals.

Finally . . .

So many people I've had in workshops seem to think they have little aptitude for design and can't draw. Whenever you make stuff, remember that your personal style will emerge unless it's rigorously contained. The way you set about a project, your personal quirks using tools, and any decoration you might apply will inevitably stamp everything you make as yours. If you're worried about a lack of drawing skills when it comes to finishing dolls, get some small children to help. They'll think anything you do is wonderful. Teenagers may be less charitable, of course.

MARKER LINE. Markers are great for adding fine lines or even spirals.

RECOMMENDED FURTHER READING

WOODTURNING TECHNIQUE
Raffan, Richard. *Turning Wood with Richard Raffan 3rd Edition*
(The Taunton Press, 2008)

Raffan, Richard. *Taunton's Complete Illustrated Guide to Turning*
(The Taunton Press, 2005)

SETTING UP
Bird, Lonnie. *The Bandsaw Book*
(The Taunton Press, 1999)

Nagyszalanczy, Sandor. *Woodshop Dust Control*
(The Taunton Press, 1996)

SHARPENING
Lee, Leonard. *The Complete Guide to Sharpening*
(The Taunton Press, 1995)

FINISHES
Jewitt, Jeff. *Taunton's Complete Illustrated Guide to Finishing*
(The Taunton Press, 2004)

Dresdner, Michael. *The New Wood Finishing Book*
(The Taunton Press, 1999)

OTHER RICHARD RAFFAN BOOKS
Turning Bowls with Richard Raffan
(The Taunton Press, 2002)

Turning Boxes with Richard Raffan
(The Taunton Press, 2002)

Turning Projects with Richard Raffan
(The Taunton Press, 1991)

The Art of Turned Bowls
(The Taunton Press, 2008)

RICHARD RAFFAN DVDs
Turning Wood with Richard Raffan
(The Taunton Press, 2003)

Turning Boxes with Richard Raffan
(The Taunton Press, 2003)

Turning Projects with Richard Raffan
(The Taunton Press, 2003)

The New Turning Wood with Richard Raffan
(The Taunton Press, 2008)

Turning Bowls
(The Taunton Press, 2009)

INDEX

Note: Page numbers in *italics* indicate projects.

A

Abrasives, 15, 27
Axle options, 41

B

Balance tray, *159–65*
Bandsaws, 15–16, 20–21
Bilboquet, *146–51*
    about: overview of game and project, 146
    tethering ball to cup, 150–51 (*see also*
        Spheres)
    turning cup and handle, 147–49
Blanks, preparing, 21
Book overview, 2–3
Bug. *See* Wheely bug
Burning wood, 178–79

C

Calipers, 16
Car. *See* Racing car
Carving, 179
Catches, tool, 28–29
CBN (cubic boron nitride) wheel, sharpening
        tools on, 9–12
Center punches, 16
Chamfered chuck jaws, 14–15
Chamfers, sanding, 110
Choking hazards, 5–6
Chuck keys, 24
Chucks, 13–15. *See also* Re-chucking
Coloring wood, 180–82
Cones, turning wheels between, 46–48
Croquet set, *115–21*
    about: overview of game rules and pieces,
        115–17
    turning mallet handle, 118–19
    turning mallet head, 117
    turning/painting post, 120–21
Cross-grained wheels, 49–53
Cylinders, turning. *See* Turning cylinders and
        dowels

D

Depth gauge, simple, 134
Dowels, turning. *See* Turning cylinders and
        dowels
Dust control/collection, 12, 24

E

Ear protection, 24
Enclosed-axle wheels, 42–45
Endgrain
    avoiding catches on, 28–29
    squaring, 33–34
Eye protection, 24, 81

F

Face shield, 24
Finishing touches
    burning, 178–79
    carving, 179
    coloring, 180–82
    finishes, 176–77
Food-safe finishes, 176–77
Friction, for blackening wood, 178
Fruit and vegetables to "cut," *106–14*
    about: overview of project, 106–07
    fixing magnets and Velcro, 108–09
    safety precaution, 107
    shaping knife, 112–14
    turning pieces sliced across, 107–10
    turning pieces sliced end to end, 111–12
Furniture, recycling wood from, 18–19

G

Goblet, *139–45*
Gouges, 8–9, 10–12, 28
Grinding wheel, sharpening tools on, 9–12

K

Knife, shaping, 112–14

L

Lathes. *See also Turning references*
    chucks for, 13–15
    dust control/collection, 12
    listening to, 27
    safety tips, 22–23, 24–25
    setting up, 12–13, 30–31
    speed control, 24, 30–31
    tool rest, 12, 27
    unattended, safety, 24
    vibration control, 12, 25
    where to stand/stance, 25, 26
Logs, 19–20

M

Magnets
    fixing/aligning, 108–09
    safety precaution, 6
Marker pens, for coloring wood, 182
Measuring tools, 16
Metal (soft), turning, 86

N

Nesting tubs, *131–38*
    about: overview of project, 131
    choosing wood, 132–33
    turning cross-grain tubs, 133–38
    turning endgrain tubs, 138

O

Oil and wax finishes, 176
Omnibus, open-air, *71*
1-2-3 Rule, 28
Open-air omnibus, *71*

P

Painting (coloring) wood, 180–82
Peggies, *72–79*
    about: overview of project, 72–73
    artwork, 78–79
    size and wood, 73
    turning, 74–78
Poles, sectioned, 173
Posts, turning, 171–74
Projects
    about: finishing. *See* Finishing touches; your
        personal style and, 182
    balance tray, *159-65*
    bilboquet, *146-51*
    croquet set, *115-21*
    fruit and vegetables to "cut," *106-14*
    goblet, *139-45*
    nesting tubs, *131-38*
    open-air omnibus, *71*
    peggies, *72-79*
    racing car, *65-71*
    snails, pair of, *64*
    spheres, *98-105*
    spinning tops, *152-58*
    stackers, *88-97*
    table skittles, *166-75*
    teether and rattle, *122-30*
    wands, *80-87*

wheely bug, 56–63
Punches, spring, 16

R

Racing car, *65–71*
   about: overview of project, 65–66
   adding wheels and driver, 70
   open-air omnibus variation, *71*
   turning body, 66–70
Rattle. *See* Teether and rattle
Re-chucking, 96
Rulers, 16

S

Safety, 4–7, 24–25
   blunt sharp points, 6–7
   choking hazards, 5–6
   chuck key, 24
   dust collection, 24
   ear protection, 24
   face and eye protection, 24, 81
   lathe operation, 24–25
   magnets and, 6
   perspective on, 4–5
   power saw precautions, 107, 125
   shop basics, 22–23
   size, scale, weight and, 7
   smooth surfaces for, 6
   for toddlers, 5–7
   tool catches (and avoiding them), 28–29
   unattended machines, 24
   vibration control, 12, 25
Sanders, 15
Saws, 15–16, 22–23
Scale, of toys, 7
Scrapers, 8–9, 10, 27, 28
Sharp points, 6–7
Sharpening tools
   on CBN wheel, 9–12
   first steps, 10
   gouges, 10–12
   importance of, 27
   scrapers and skews, 10
Size, of toys, 7
Skew chisels, 8–9, 10, 29
Skittles. *See* Table skittles
Smoothness, of surfaces, 6
Snails, pair of, *64*
Solitaire sets, 99
Spheres, *98–105*
   about: overview of turning, 98–99
   drilling, 127
   turning freehand, 99–103
   turning with jig, 104–05
Spinning tops, *152–58*
Splits, in wood, 20, 22
Spring dividers, 16
Stackers, *88–97*

about: overview of project, 88–89
   making rings, 93–95
   making tube, 92–93
   preparing blanks, 89
   re-chucking to change shapes, 96, 97
   turning base, 90–92
   turning center post and head, 96

T

Table skittles, *166–75*
   about: game variations, 175; overview of
      game and project, 166
   assembling, 175
   turning base, 167–70
   turning cap, 170–71
   turning knocker and pins, 174–75
   turning post, 171–74
Teether and rattle, *122–30*
   about: overview of project, 122–23
   drilling spheres, 127
   turning rattle, 128–30
   turning teether, 123–26
Tool rest, 12, 27
Tools, 8–16. *See also* Lathes
   abrasives and sanders, 15
   gouges, skew chisels, scrapers, 8–9
   measuring, 16
   safe operation. *See* Safety
   saws, 15–16
   sharpening, 9–12, 27
Tops, spinning, *152–58*
Torch, for burning wood, 178–79
Turning cylinders and dowels, 30–39
   lathe setup and speeds, 30–31
   setting diameter, 34–36
   square to round, 31–32
   squaring endgrain, 32–34
   thin dowels, 36–39
   truing cylinder size, 34–36
Turning soft metal, 86
Turning wheels, 40–53
   about: overview of, 40–41
   axle options and, 41
   between cones, 46–48
   cross-grained wheels, 49–53
   enclosed-axle wheels, 42–45
   wheel design, 41–42
Turning wood. *See also* Lathes
   basics, 27
   hand support, 82
   ideal cutting angle, 26, 27
   listening to lathe, 27
   moving with tool, 27
   preventing flexing, 82
   sectioned poles, 173
   tool catches (and avoiding them), 28–29
   tool rest height, 27

V

Vegetables. *See* Fruit and vegetables to "cut"
Velcro, fixing, 109
Vibration control, 12, 25
Visors, 24

W

Wands, *80–87*
   about: overview of project, 80–82
   turning, 82–87
   types of, illustrated, 80–81
Wax and oil finishes, 176
Weight, of toys, 7
Wheels, turning. *See* Turning wheels
Wheely bug, *56–63*
   about: overview of project, 56–57
   stringing segments, adding eyes, 62–63
   turning axle, 61
   turning body, 57–58
   turning tail, 58–59
   turning/fitting wheels, 60–62
Wood
   about: overview of, 17
   air-dried vs. kiln-dried, 19
   from arborists, 19–20
   blanks, preparing, 21
   cost considerations, 20–21
   defects in, 22
   finishing. *See* Finishing touches
   hardness, 20
   at hardwood dealers, 18
   at home centers/lumberyards, 18
   logs, 19–20
   in recycled furniture, 18–19
   in shop, 19
   size options, 18, 19, 20–21
   splits in, 20, 22
   types of, 18
   what to look for, 20–21
   where to find, 18–20
   at woodworking retailers, 18

If you like this book, you'll love *Fine Woodworking.*